RECALIBRATE

EQUIPPING GOD'S PEOPLE TO SHAPE THEIR WORLD

JONATHAN SQUIRRELL

Kingdom
Breakthrough

For Paige

And with grateful thanks to all who learned alongside us at the Beacon School of Supernatural Life (2017-2020)

CONTENTS

Part III

OUR ACTIVITY

Part IV

OUR LEADING

Part V
MOVING FORWARD

THE CHALLENGE

COVID has challenged our world in remarkable ways. Jesus-followers, and those who claim no faith, have had to adapt. Change is seldom easy, what we would have imagined, or even wanted.

How can we transition when we sense the old has gone but its replacement is unclear?

Our culture is solution focussed and we long for answers. The journey appears less important than the destination. Yet, as followers of Jesus, our relationship with Him is one of companionship, not knowledge.

It's great to learn and expand our horizons, but our pilgrimage is a lifetime of walking with Jesus. From that perspective, church is peripheral (and much of 'church' as we have known it, perhaps irrelevant). But in terms of meaningful growth with other disciples, church is essential.

As we walk with Jesus individually, we talk with Him and learn His heart for the world and for us. The collective experience of such journeying is church. A desire to know Him better can replace our obsession with answers.

The Bible is neither rule book nor history, but a pointer to Jesus. We read the Scriptures to move us closer to their author, not for answers. Then, in God's grace, we discover that a relationship is more important than a solution.

In these strangest of times, God is nudging His people. We can pause and evaluate. The Father's voice rings clear because we have taken the time to listen. He has lots to say.

For now, park your questions about church and lean instead into Jesus. He clarifies what is necessary when we need to know.

Embrace relationship. Meditate on Matthew 11:28-30. Read it in several modern translations (use biblegateway.com) and chew it over. Jesus will replace our weariness and our burdens.

Walk with Him, join other pilgrims en route, and you will find rest for your souls.

> *Consider him who endured such opposition from sinners, so that you will not grow weary and lose heart.* (Hebrews 12:3)

PREFACE

For my wife Paige and myself, our experience of leading a long-term discipleship school taught us a great deal about God and about us! The impact on the attendees was significant. It surprised those who had read little since high school that contemporary Christian writing could change their lives. Those nervous about public speaking received confidence to stand in front of others and share testimony of God's goodness. Practical sessions on the streets and in post-service prayer ministry equipped every participant and both of the leaders.

This book springs from reworking our curriculum and adding extra material. In almost every chapter, I appreciate authors have written whole books on these topics. One could always write more. I pray that *Recalibrate* will encourage readers to think again and make whatever changes God prompts. If this book acts as a launchpad for renewal and further exploration, I have succeeded.

You may read *Recalibrate* as a standalone text. Together with the Study Guide, the book will provide material for 26 weeks of teaching, approximately one academic year. In that scenario, attendees may wish to read the relevant chapter in the book before each week's session. Leaders can then use the Study Guide as an outline.

Studying together is by far the most powerful way to understand and apply the text. I have included many Scriptures in full and made reference to others, sometimes in the endnotes. Take these words from God and pray them over your life and ministry.

Naturally, the audio book is simply an audio version of the printed book.

I have given credit to other authors and speakers for quotations wherever possible. If I have missed one, please let me know through our website (kingdombreakthrough.org) and I will correct the text.

May God bless you to become more like Jesus.

Comments from previous participants:

- "'If you want to walk on water you must get out of the boat'. This school turned my life around and started me on a journey with my Heavenly Father that will never be the same."
- "The school is a journey of both development and discovery: discover your true identity in Christ; develop a deeper intimacy with God; develop a deeper fellowship with other believers; discover and develop your spiritual gifts. The school will help you learn, and live out, the values of the Kingdom of Heaven—helping you to walk in the power of the Holy Spirit."
- "The school opened new horizons, leaving the lies of the past behind and walking into the truth of everything God has planned for me. It's believing that there are

opportunities to be Jesus to others, praying and sharing what God has done and what He can do."

- "The school with Jonathan and Paige is the best discipleship course, with which I have been involved, during the last 30 years!"

- "Applying for the school was a great decision. Paige and Jonathan encouraged and gently pushed me beyond my comfort zone giving me the opportunity to explore, share, feed into others while at the same time growing in intimacy and revelation with our Heavenly Father. Each week was a new adventure."

- "I found the school enriching, challenging, and even at times a bit scary but I grew closer to God, gained more confidence in a God of might and possibilities. I had very negative things happen in people close to me at the time and it enabled me to manage and offer support instead of feeling helpless. I strongly recommend making time for this."

- "I learned new habits to experience the continual presence of God."

- "Though I have been a Christian for many years and received a lot of teaching and training I found the course faith building, spiritually inspiring, healthily challenging to my comfort zones and well presented by Jonathan and Paige, I highly recommend it!"

- "The school was faith provoking, and really helpful in affirming my identity in Christ. It was great to do it with others as we learnt from one another, and also supported each other with the activations."

INTRODUCTION

Few people take time to consider how modern church reflects the heart of God, or ponder expressing worship differently. There are stages in our lives when we have such an opportunity. COVID is a case in point, but there are also other seasons when we may pause long enough to ask what church is all about. Whenever you read this book, you have God's permission to take stock and to readjust.

THINK AGAIN

In 2009, Paige and I took up the leadership of an existing church. But we understood we needed to start again if we wanted to see a fresh move of God. With a genuine sense of stepping into the unknown, we thanked God for everything that He had accomplished over the previous 150 years and planted a new church expression. You may believe you do not have this choice, but I suggest a reboot is essential for many churches. Now, with circumstances unprecedented in our lifetimes, we can ask God for a fresh start.

In 2021, a gradual release from COVID lockdown restrictions by the UK central government allowed six individuals to meet indoors. This rediscovered freedom reminded us that God can work with small numbers of people.

Large buildings and paid staff are unnecessary for God's kingdom to grow. The Lord has set the stage for a return to a simpler but profound faith, one that depends on community and lifelong discipleship, not mass gatherings.

We bought into the lie that bigger is always better. There is no doubt that large conferences and get-togethers have been rich experiences, but God works in small groups too. We created unsustainable, human-centred organisations. Perhaps we hoped they would be superior replacements for simple groups of world-changing Jesus-followers, but we lost the truth that simplicity is key.

THIS BOOK

The pages below offer material to begin or continue a godly review of the local church and the Kingdom of God. The book has several parts, considering the context of community, discipleship, and how to move forward. We must resist comparison with others. Instead, we ask what God is saying, and we follow His call.

34 chapters correlate to 26 teaching and practical sessions, where we look together at the Word of God through the lens of His Spirit. We allow Him to change us and then live godly lives that will honour Jesus, who loved us and gave Himself for us (Galatians 2:20).

You may have read Leonard Ravenhill's 1959 classic, *Why Revival Tarries*.[1] The book challenges the modern reader as much as ever. His tombstone asks,

> Are the things you are living for worth Christ dying for?

> — LEONARD RAVENHILL

This is a wake-up call for the contemporary church. Are our values God's values? Have we missed out on His purposes because we loved 'churchianity' instead of Christ?

Earlier, I considered calling this book 'Colonies of Heaven'. I first heard this phrase when studying the first millennium Celtic saints, who also coined the term 'villages of God'. In both cases, they established communities that together *lived* the Kingdom of God.

The Celts practised discipleship as a way of life, much of which was mundane existence. There was nothing romantic in the challenges of the seventh century: war, disease and relentless daily grind caused untold suffering. And yet, God was at work.

Today, we must recapture the simplicity of an older approach. We long to see Jesus-followers *be church* in local communities and workplaces. As we read, pray and worship together, God knits us into 'Colonies of Heaven'.

For this to happen, we need fresh understandings of community and lifelong discipleship. We recognise following Jesus is not a programme but a process. Discipleship is a life-calling that enables us to bring out the 'God-colours' and 'God-flavours' of our world (Matthew 5:13-14 MSG).

OVER COMPLICATION

About 12 years ago, a friend asked about my goals for this new church. My response was clear: *church that works*. Through my personal journey and listening to varied reports from other people, I realised that our experiences of the church are mixed.

In part, we live disappointed lives because we have imported complexity into the local church. We understand these are challenging days and there is much we do not know. However, our faith is simple to follow. Why do we complicate everything?

Earlier in the COVID pandemic, physical separation was a significant barrier to fellowship. Most of our previous experiences occurred with other people. This forced me to address this question: *what is a local church at its irreducible minimum?* Do we need a band, or PA, or coffee, or a pastor/minister/vicar, or...?

When we strip everything else away, we retain a much simpler list of constituent parts. I conducted this 'essentials' exercise with other church leadership teams, and near the top of most lists was fellowship. This is unsurprising, since we have all missed seeing one another for so long. We acknowledge services do not equal fellowship. What we all yearn for is a simple, workable community.

Worship, teaching, prayer, support and other items are also important. They all fit into a paradigm of a church that is centred on biblical discipleship taught, demonstrated, and lived out supernaturally in sustainable community settings. I appreciate that the word supernatural can conjure up extremes and perhaps remind us of unhelpful previous experiences. But Jesus is supernatural, our salvation is supernatural, and so is heaven. God enables the lives of all Jesus-followers to be *above* the natural or normal.

Supernatural does not have to mean strange. It can simply be that our unconscious reaction to an accident or illness is to pray instead of panic. This is a worthwhile goal for every follower of Jesus, irrespective of age.

Is it too much for us to believe that this could provide much needed meaningful fellowship, facilitate personal spiritual growth and encourage outreach in the most natural ways? This allows us to be the church that Jesus died for without the trappings that have so often played a large and distracting part in our coming together.

STRIPPING AWAY THE PROPS

Earlier, I used the word *sustainable*. As a paid pastor, I appreciated a regular stipend brings financial security. It is an attractive idea! But when we came to realise that employment costs consumed a huge percentage of our church income, we knew it was wrong for us to continue. I cannot overemphasise this was a very personal decision and want no one in a paid position to feel that they must follow our example.

However, now that a ministerial role is no longer a financial burden on the church, we have released funds for ministry. Groups without buildings do not need to allocate funds for premises maintenance, either. Perhaps the perceived requirement of paid staff and purpose-built buildings has blinded us to the reality that church is nothing about pastors, premises or programmes! It is all about Jesus; following Him, becoming like Him, and encouraging others.

That is a church that works.

This raises practical and personal questions for paid staff and for those fellowships that have property. Some issues are difficult to resolve. I know that from experience. But perhaps the greatest conviction came when I received a revelation about 'every member' ministry. I have believed in this for years and preached it. However, I modelled the 'ministry of the few'.

THE MINISTRY OF THE MANY

From 2017 to lockdown, we ran a School of Supernatural Life. During that period, God equipped people from our church and others in the area to be disciples. Each week we taught from the Bible, demonstrated the Kingdom, equipped the saints and released them into ministry. Everyone grew, including us. We proved that 'every member' ministry works. And yet I still practised the opposite.

I believe in leadership. Not everybody can do everything. However, more people can reach their God-given potential.

And so I stepped down to make way for others to grow, lead, surprise even themselves and watch as Jesus built His church. Many others before us have realised that staff and premises are not prerequisites. This is nothing new. We are arguing for a simpler, older approach, one that is based on the lives of Jesus-followers in their locality. This is less 'gathered church' and more 'local church'. It includes discipleship as a lifestyle, caught as well as taught, as we share life together.

We can use buildings for a variety of purposes. The occasional coming together of small groups needs space, and church premises provide this facility. But there are also ingenious ways to connect Jesus-followers to the local community. Many churches already host a food bank. Others meet particular local needs. It is possible that the only decent sized building in the vicinity may be the church building. Could other groups use these premises in ways that show that God is calling everyone everywhere to Himself? This may not be traditionally evangelistic, but it is incarnational.

CHALLENGES

Three particular challenges present themselves when we consider staff and property. First, it is easy for ministers to look to their stipend for financial security instead of God. Second, they may 'need to be needed' by the congregation. *What is my identity if I am not the pastor?* Stepping away from a position requires leaders to be secure in their identity in Christ. They will need great courage. Others will misunderstand them. Third, whilst we reiterate the truth that church is people, not buildings, there is an understandable connection with something physical that can be hard to leave, especially when we associate particular memories with buildings.

It is easy to equate church with meetings or services. Although such corporate times have been profitable, they play a minor role in the spiritual life of a believer. Larger meetings when small groups come together can occur less frequently, freeing up disciples from too many periods of *organised* worship and releasing a building to be used by other groups.

Church that works, therefore, needs to be uncomplicated in structure, Jesus-centred and focussed on lifelong discipleship. This is possible when we take the spotlight off ourselves and focus on Jesus. Robin Mark's song[2] is a good anthem for this season:

Jesus, all for Jesus, all I am and have and ever hope to be.

— ROBIN MARKS

Like so much else in life, our aspirations can fall short but we must do more than *try*. Putting Jesus first has to become a reality. The writer of the letter to the Hebrews summarised in 12:2,

Let us fix our eyes on Jesus, the author and perfecter of our faith…

How do we refocus? The answer is in the previous verse:

Let us throw off everything that hinders and the sin that so easily entangles, and let us run with perseverance the race marked out for us.

We become aware that we are in a spiritual battle against a real enemy. He wants nothing more than a divided church full of disgruntled believers. Then we understand that our fellow Jesus-followers are not the opposition.

In addition, we throw off anything that hinders, including our experiences that often feed into our expectations of what the church *should* be like. And we run towards Jesus. We do not follow a path of our choosing, but what He has already marked for us.

As we set out on the discipleship journey, built on the Bible, lived in the power of the Holy Spirit and enjoyed in the meaningful company of others, the future is bright. We have hope for the present and for eternity.

> *Be filled with the Spirit. Speak to one another with psalms, hymns, and spiritual songs. Sing and make music in your heart to the Lord, always giving thanks to God the Father for everything, in the name of our Lord Jesus Christ.* (Ephesians 5:18b-20)

PART I
OUR CONTEXT

1

THE FAMILY OF JESUS

Over the next few chapters, we will examine the role of community in the lives of Jesus-followers. What is it and why is it central to God's plan for His church? What about numbers, leadership and evangelistic growth?

FAMILY

God has designed us to thrive within a family context. Whilst many people cannot experience the support of a healthy nuclear family, often through no fault of their own, this remains God's best. For the isolated, God's family is vital.

> *God sets the lonely in **families**.* (Psalm 68:6)

This is also true for disciples who are the only believing members in their immediate family, and for those who are blessed to live in very supportive environments. 'God's family' is another way of referring to other Christians, as these passages indicate:

> *Therefore, as we have opportunity, let us do good to all people,*

*especially to those who belong to the **family of believers**.*
(Galatians 6:10)

For this reason, I kneel before the Father, from whom his whole
   ***family in heaven and on earth** derives its name.*
   (Ephesians 3:14-15)

*And in fact, you do love all of **God's family** throughout*
   Macedonia. (1 Thessalonians 4:10)

*Show proper respect to everyone, love the **family of believers**,*
   fear God, honour the emperor. (1 Peter 2:17)

Resist [the devil], standing firm in the faith, because you know
   *that the **family of believers** throughout the world is*
   undergoing the same kind of sufferings. (1 Peter 5:9)

God is the Father, and we are the children. It is as simple as that.
His family, coming together as local followers of Jesus, provides
the nourishing context for discipleship to flourish. When church
gets too big, however, it is much harder for a family atmosphere
to be sustained. Many small churches lament their lack of
numbers because they feel they cannot 'do what large churches
can do'. But the modest size can be a real benefit when we
consider that God's commission—to make disciples—will only
work in small groups. Remember what Jesus said:

Therefore, go and make disciples of all nations, baptising them in
   the name of the Father and of the Son and of the Holy Spirit,
   and teaching them to obey everything I have commanded you.
   (Matthew 28:19-20)

This does not require large numbers, but obedience to the call of
Christ.

LEAD LIKE JESUS

Just as families work best when there is an element of leadership, so in the church we need those who model servant leadership:

> *For even the Son of Man did not come to be served, but to serve, and to give his life as a ransom for many.* (Mark 10:45)

If the leader serves, drawing out the best from everyone present, then all participants will flourish. There is no need for one person to do everything but all learn together. And as others watch us honour one another, they will want to join in. Evangelism is the natural outworking of a shared life and becomes the shared responsibility of the group.

2

NUMERICAL GROWTH

Much has been said and written about numbers, size and the growth of individuals and groups. How do we recalibrate our thinking?

DEPTH AND WIDTH

There are several biblical considerations when we consider numbers.

> [Prayer for all people] is good, and pleases God our Saviour, who wants all people to be saved and to come to a knowledge of the truth. (1 Timothy 2:1-4)

Such salvation is only available through Jesus (John 14:6; Acts 4:12) and He died for everyone. Therefore, it is natural and right for us to desire that everyone comes to Him. Numbers are important because every number is a person. Equally,

> It was [Jesus] who gave some to be apostles, some to be prophets, some to be evangelists, and some to be pastors and teachers, to prepare God's people for works of service, so that the body of

Christ may be built up ... and become mature, attaining to the whole measure of the fulness of Christ. Then we will no longer be infants, tossed back and forth ... Instead ... we will in all things grow up ... (Ephesians 4:11-15)

God wants His children to be grown up in their walk with Him. This is not a matter of physical age, but concerns spiritual depth. We may know mature younger people and immature seniors. God is looking for disciples rather than non-discipled converts. Therefore, following the command of Jesus (Matthew 28:19-20), we must discern how to reach the world whilst ensuring that those who acknowledge Jesus also *grow* in Him.

It is relatively easy to enter the number of professions of faith on a spreadsheet. Maturity is much harder to measure. Would we rather have a large church congregation or a mature one? Most of us would like both! But maturity is the goal—that is the commission that Jesus has given us.

Then, as Jesus-followers mature and become more like Him, they are attractive to others too. If we are part of a larger group or church, there is nothing to stop us spending more time in smaller meetings that promote every-person ministry. Thus, we grow in width and depth at the same time.

HOW MANY IS ENOUGH?

There are several events that work best with larger numbers. Are such activities necessary for church to still function? If they are important, then we can consider decreasing their frequency. For example, it can be a wonderful experience for a whole church to share a meal together. But if small groups eat with one another weekly, we can then organise a corporate meal every couple of months.

A larger setting for shared worship encourages everyone; small groups can replicate a simplified version of this as talents, equipment and inclination permit, and then join with other groups, perhaps each month, for a shared service.

In these scenarios, we need only a handful of people to meet together regularly for fellowship, prayer, study, teaching and fun. The size may depend on the number of local Jesus-followers and the facilities—some houses are bigger than others. Likewise, outside venues may determine numbers and coffee shops, pub function rooms and other places may suit.

There is no magic number, but the reality is simple. To allow everyone to take part, we cannot get too big. Each group will determine when some members may initiate another group. I will consider this further in Chapter 4.

A LITTLE MORE ABOUT DEPTH

Every follower of Jesus must assess their walk with God. *Who am I in comparison with a year ago?* Remember, we are comparing only with ourselves at an earlier stage, never with others. As we walk with Jesus, natural progress is inevitable. If, on close examination, we believe our lives are much the same, we can ask God for His insight on why this may be. Then we can take corrective action.

In Psalm 1:1-3, the psalmist writes:

> *Blessed is the man who does not walk in the counsel of the wicked*
> *or stand in the way of sinners or sit in the seat of mockers.*
> *But his delight is in the law of the LORD, and on his law he*
> *meditates day and night. He is like a tree planted by streams*
> *of water, which yields its fruit in season and whose leaf does*
> *not wither. Whatever he does prospers.*

Here, lifestyle choices influence our relationship with God. Spiritual depth will only characterise our lives if we are intentional about putting God first. We take advice from Him instead of prevailing opinion. Our actions are compatible with the Bible and godly living. We focus on what God is saying, and that provides meaningful sustenance. This process takes time, but gradually, we realise our priorities are changing. God draws us to Himself more than to our surroundings. We know that the fruitfulness of our lives is pleasing to God—we are truly following Jesus.

And when we get it wrong, we are quick to sort things out:

> *If we confess our sins, he is faithful and just and will forgive us our sins and purify us from all unrighteousness.* (1 John 1:9)

Keeping right with God is a characteristic of a life following Him. Our words and actions are consistent. And when we combine our personal walk in God's presence, with our walk with those around us, we

> *spur one another on towards love and good deeds* (Hebrews 10:24)

We act as catalysts for one another. Community works.

Is it better to be 'deep' in our walk with God or 'wide' in our numbers? The answer is both. But as our numbers increase, we need the 'iron sharpening iron' of others close to us. That may mean additional small groups. What a problem to have!

3

LEADERSHIP

Like the donkey in the animated film *Shrek*, we long to be chosen. Whether our role is to follow or to lead, how do we work this out in a Jesus honouring way?

JESUS-LEADERSHIP

Bill Hybels said that the future of the church rests primarily in the hands of its leaders.[1] Leadership is vital in every area and church is no different. At their best, leaders champion their followers, supporting and encouraging them to achieve their potential. When leadership is authoritarian, it devalues and crushes people. If you journey in Christian circles for any length of time, you may have experienced both extremes and everything in between.

Godly leaders are key if church is to work. They may, however, look quite different from what we have seen modelled in the past.

Some churches have operated with a plurality of leadership and others have embraced either a first among equals approach or one person in charge. Given the variety of our backgrounds, the expectations of both congregations and leaders can be very different, resulting in various degrees of conflict. Let us examine the example of Jesus. Then we can apply His teaching to small, local gatherings and then, by extension, to the local church.

We have already seen how Jesus came to serve (Mark 10:45). The sacrificial servant figure of Isaiah 53:2-9 also speaks volumes into leadership that embraces suffering and reflects the heart of the master leader, Jesus.

> *He grew up before him like a tender shoot, and like a root out of dry ground. He had no beauty or majesty to attract us to him, nothing in his appearance that we should desire him.*
> *He was despised and rejected by mankind, a man of suffering, and familiar with pain.*
> *Like one from whom people hide their faces, he was despised, and we held him in low esteem.*
> *Surely, he took up our pain and bore our suffering, yet we considered him punished by God, stricken by him, and afflicted.*
> *But he was pierced for our transgressions, he was crushed for our iniquities; the punishment that brought us peace was on him, and by his wounds, we are healed.*
> *We all, like sheep, have gone astray ... and the LORD has laid on him the iniquity of us all.*
> *He was oppressed and afflicted, yet he did not open his mouth; he was led like a lamb to the slaughter ... By oppression and judgement he was taken away ... He was assigned a grave with the wicked ...*

We long for such leaders, both at the smaller gatherings and the larger groupings. It is the character that each of us should emulate. What is important to Jesus must become important to us. If you read this passage and it impacts your life because of all that your Saviour did for you, then you position yourself well to follow His example.

This is what the church needs, regardless of the size. The world yearns to see leadership that is not self-centred, whose statements are trustworthy, and whose promises are genuine. Church can be the safest place, though recent events have shouted the opposite. It is therefore our responsibility to tell another story.

CONTROL

Ungodly, human control is unhelpful, but a good leader can provide security and safety, nudging people along and drawing out their best without ever resorting to manipulation. All groups are different and no leaders are identical in their outworking of servant leadership. That is as it should be. What is a constant factor, however, is these leaders' desire to follow Jesus and lead like Him.

We need wisdom to deal with genuine questions and also the humility to acknowledge that none of us has all the answers. That honesty frees up the enquirer and guards against control on the part of the leader. A certain self-awareness is important too. If you appreciate you have the strongest personality and the loudest voice in a group, it is essential you do not dominate discussion. Bring out the thoughts of others. Allow the quieter ones to take part.

A final safeguard is to ensure that all are secure in their God-given identity. This is a key part of the teaching in the next Part of this book and I cannot overestimate its importance. Some leaders exercise control because they are fearful: *if I do not take charge, this will reflect badly on my leadership*. But we need to remember that we do not base our identity on our view of ourselves, our job title, or even our role. We are 'us' because of Jesus. That is it. When I am secure in that identity, it does not matter how I perform, what people call me, or what I feel. There is no need to exercise control.

Good leadership knows when to take hard decisions, to lead people along uncomfortable paths and sometimes deal with troublesome people. Overbearing control is another matter.

SMALL GROUP, LARGER MEETINGS AND CHURCH

At the small group level, there is less need for traditional forms of leadership. There needs be co-ordination, of course, a little organisation in terms of dates, times and venues. But small groups facilitate whole life discipleship as we share everyday things as much as time and individual circumstances allow. Even as we read and study the Bible together, it is important for everyone to take part and to pray. *Facilitation* is the key word in this context.

When small groups combine for larger or whole church events, we require a little greater leadership. There is more to organise. However, we still want to model the 'ministry of everyone', sensitive to the needs of greater numbers and other constraints.

Whatever the size of meeting and whatever its frequency, servant leadership points to Jesus and encourages each follower to grow in a place of safety.

4

GROWING DEEP AND WIDE

An old children's song reminds us that

There's a fountain flowing deep and wide.

— SIDNEY E. COX (1887-1975)

I have also heard it said that church health in some areas may be described as a mile wide but only an inch deep. There is clearly something worth probing a little further in this area of depth and width. We may have a small number of people, but they may be 'big' people in the sense of spiritual maturity.

THE GROWTH WITHIN GROUPS

Existing church life can be inward looking. We may accuse leaders of focussing so intently on the existing congregation that little time or energy is available for those outside. Whatever our experience, all would doubtless agree that our walk with God is worth sharing. What part can small groups play in evangelism?

Groups expand when others join. Often this is transfer growth by other believers; initially, this is how we establish groups. But as our shared life settles down and we experience its value, there is room to encourage others to join us. If a regular meal is part of our collective time, inviting a neighbour, friend or colleague is very natural. Food is great for disarming the sceptical or hostile enquirer. The goal is relationship with other group members. The invitation may be, *come on a journey with us.*

Discipleship is a lifelong process. For many of us, growing up in traditional church has blinded us to this reality and we are also unaware of our church's sub culture. Rather than inviting people to leave their own environment and join an alien alternative, the great advantage of using homes is that they are natural extensions of ourselves. Homes and houses differ. But they all provide shelter and a safe place. Through COVID, we have realised once more that so often people yearn for human contact. Isolation is hard and sometimes perfect strangers have the most remarkable conversations. We are uncertain whether 'getting back to normal' will ever happen and how short-lived this desire for company may be. For now, it is very real.

Church experience has disillusioned many. The faith of some may be intact, but people are wary of organised religion. For others, they have slipped away from belief and practice. How wonderful if God would use small groups of normal, everyday people living honest and open lives to restore those who have slipped through the cracks. I believe there is an untapped army of broken soldiers whom we can love back into active service.

The bar for joining such a community meal or activity should be low. A certain openness to spiritual matters is important for prayer and study, of course. But otherwise we embrace the sceptical through invitation to *travel together and see where it will lead us!* That is much more disarming than inviting others to join our club when they do not understand all we believe. It also reflects the way of Jesus.

When He leaves for Galilee in John 1:43, Jesus tells Philip to follow Him. Philip then finds his friend Nathanael and explains that he has met the Messiah. Nathanael is sceptical when he hears Jesus is from Nazareth and Philip invites Nathanael to

Come and see. (John 1:46)

As a result, Nathanael believes.

We do not need to answer every question, but invite people to meet Jesus. He understands them. Since we ourselves are on a journey of discovery—we have not 'arrived'—we can invite others to join us. These newcomers may already be Jesus-followers. Either way, we would love to walk together and see where Jesus takes us.

HOW GROUPS REPRODUCE

As group numbers increase, there will be the opportunity to start new small communities. In this manner, it is easy to see how groups may saturate an area. It would work well in both urban and rural environments. As with everything else, there is no one way to reproduce groups. Some may work best with people from a particular area; in other cases, shared interests may delineate a group. Age, life stage or indeed anything else may be the trigger to start. However, over time, what keeps people together is a common spiritual connection.

Additional groups need co-ordinators, but remember, this may be as simple as deciding time and venue for the next meeting!

SOCIETAL CHANGE

Let us take a moment to dream. First, in geographical terms, we can view followers of Jesus scattered throughout city and countryside. There may be a number in a particular home, but even then, that household may enjoy limited influence. However, when the households come together, the potential for neighbourhood change increases. Over time, one home cannot accommodate so many attendees. Another group begins in a neighbouring street or village. And then another. The influence spreads. As a result, we impact society.

Second, local interest groups connect with others who share their passion. Before long, people notice that there is something different about them.

Neither of these ideas are novel and Jesus-followers already model them in several places. It is challenging for us in traditional models of meeting. We have spent so long in 'doing church' we have neither the energy nor the enthusiasm for 'being church'.

God is calling us to something new. This will undoubtedly look different from what we have experienced historically. But what God is calling us into requires courage if we are to be characterised by depth and width: deep in our walk with God; wide in the influence we have on those around us.

COVID may have provided us with a unique setting for such change, but many have already grasped this opportunity. God never envisaged discipleship as a 'Lone Ranger' activity. It can only be effective in the company of others.

5

MOVING FORWARD

So let us begin. I will address the practicalities of discipleship throughout the book. For now, understand that the culture of meaningful community provides a wonderfully supportive environment for discipleship to flourish. We all long to thrive and not merely survive. For such aspiration to become a reality requires potentially hard decisions to be made. But it is abundantly worthwhile!

When is the best time to start? Right now. The need for depth and width continues. We have huge potential to influence our society. The task is urgent. So how do we move forward?

Find others who are interested in meeting together. You need a venue and an appropriate number of people. Think about the frequency of meeting. If you are already part of a local church, could you realistically add these meetings to those you already have? Wherever possible, remain in a good relationship with existing structures.

Dream and ask God to bring to you those that He wants. Are there neighbours or friends who would be interested? Are you thinking about those who live nearby or those of similar interests?

Rural population density is much less than in urban areas, so some travel may be inevitable.

Recognise that each follower of Jesus has the Spirit of God within them. God speaks, we listen to the voice of the Spirit, and we obey. In some ways, it is simple. But it may take time to attune our spiritual hearing to understand what God is saying. Be kind to yourself. Take it one step at a time. Read your Bible and talk to God; make a note of what He is saying through Scripture and prayer. It may surprise you what He is communicating!

I find the example of the boy Samuel very encouraging. He wakes one night because he hears God calling him, but because he has not yet learned to recognise God's voice, he assumes that the Prophet Eli is the one speaking. After a while, Eli realises God is calling Samuel. He advises the boy to listen once more and then respond. We can echo his words without shame:

"Speak, for your servant is listening." (1 Samuel 3:10)

Once you have one or two like-minded co-workers, pray together that the Lord will draw others to you. Be open to divine encounters and divine surprises! As your spiritual sensitivity increases, you will be more aware of God's leading and encouraged that He wishes to use you. There will be challenges ahead, but remember the words of Jesus:

"In this world, you will have trouble. But take heart! I have overcome the world." (John 16:33)

How do we complete a long journey? One step at a time.

Our focus now shifts to the lifelong process of following Jesus: discipleship.

PART II
OUR IDENTITY

6

GETTING STARTED

WHERE ARE WE GOING?

God is not just about doing the *next thing* in your life. He is often doing a *new* thing. Are you willing to perceive it (Isaiah 43)? It may be something you have never experienced before, or it may be familiar, but with God's 'this is the right time' stamp of approval.

Disciples are followers of Jesus on a lifetime apprenticeship. As I mentioned earlier, our walk with Jesus is a calling, not a course; it is a process, not a programme. Our goal in life is to do the will of the Father. That was Jesus' way:

> *"For I have come down from heaven not to do my will but to do the will of him who sent me."* (John 6:38)

That is our calling, too. Evangelism, healing and supporting others are all important, but these flow from our relationship with the Father.

SOME POINTERS FOR THE JOURNEY

Here are six challenges for our life of discipleship:

1. **Mandate**: we want to be people who naturally live the supernatural life, who are carriers of God's presence and who stay in a place of continual learning. We never graduate from discipleship school, but a teachable spirit is our passport to progress.
2. **Cost**: we will pay whatever price. A godly walk includes sacrifice.
3. **Spirit and revelation**: we need the Spirit of wisdom and revelation to know Jesus better (Ephesians 3:17); once we know Him, we experience *his mighty strength, which he exerted in Christ when he raised him from the dead* (3:19-20).
4. **Intimacy**: we win our battles in private as we conform our minds to the mind of Christ; we do not need to limit the miraculous power of God since it flows from Him through those who are intimate with His Son.
5. **Solutions**: only God has the answers to the problems of the world; since we are His friends, we can ask Him for whatever we need.
6. **Positioning**: because we are intimate friends, Jesus uniquely positions us to receive everything the Father wishes to give; we know our identity and from that place of security we serve with confidence.

7

THE LANGUAGE OF THE SPIRIT

God speaks and we listen. It's simple in some ways, but it may be harder in practice than we sometimes appreciate.

THE VOICE OF GOD

If we wish to be led by God's Spirit, we must learn to hear His voice. Here is a key text:

> "Very truly I tell you Pharisees, anyone who does not enter the sheep pen by the gate, but climbs in by some other way, is a thief and a robber. The one who enters by the gate is the shepherd of the sheep. The gatekeeper opens the gate for him, and the sheep listen to his **voice**. He **calls** his own sheep by name and leads them out. When he has brought out all his own, he goes on ahead of them, and his sheep follow him because they know his **voice**. But they will never follow a stranger; in fact, they will run away from him because **they do not recognise a stranger's voice**." Jesus used this figure of speech, but the Pharisees did not understand what he was telling them. (John 10:1-6)

There are several assumptions in this passage. First, God has a distinctive voice. This is so important if we are to have confidence in what He says. The implication is that we can confidently discern what He is saying because we recognise it is He who is speaking!

Second, He uses His voice to communicate to His children. He has a desire to be heard. He wants us to know His thoughts about every aspect of our lives. Those of us who are parents want our children to hear our words and understand our thoughts.

Third, it is possible to understand and follow God's voice. We often disbelieve we can hear from Him, and this robs many followers of Jesus. But since God is always communicating and we have His Spirit within us, we can attune our spiritual ears to hear what He is saying. This is a process that takes time and improves with practice. Do not give up on this vital aspect of your relationship with your Heavenly Father.

Fourth, knowing God's voice enables us to distinguish it from the voice of the enemy. It was often said that the best way to identify a forged banknote was to become intimately familiar with the genuine article. The more we recognise God speaking, the easier it is to understand that other 'voices' are either the enemy or our thoughts.

Some believers get very worked up over these things. Ask God to banish everything else and speak to you in an understandable way. I have already mentioned Samuel's experience (1 Samuel 3) and that is an outstanding example of learning to hear one of the many ways that the Spirit of God communicates with us.

THE SPIRIT AND THE BIBLE

Anything that we hear from God will always be consistent with the Bible. Scripture is the baseline from which we measure every-thing. We can never claim that God is telling us something contrary to the Bible, even if we feel strongly about a matter. We will consider the Bible in greater detail in the next chapter.

4 HELPFUL KEYS TO HEARING GOD'S VOICE

Based on Habakkuk 2:1-3, Mark and Patti Virkler[1] have identified scriptural principles that can help our understanding and application of God's words.

> *I will **stand at my watch and station myself on the ramparts**; I will **look to see** what he will say to me, and what answer I am to give to this complaint. Then **the LORD replied**: "**Write down the revelation and make it plain** on tablets so that a herald may run with it. For the revelation awaits an appointed time; it speaks of the end and will not prove false. Though it linger, wait for it; it will certainly come and will not delay."*

We live such hectic lives. Learning to become still before the Lord is no simple task and may involve unplugging from electronic devices and social media. There is clear intentionality in positioning oneself to hear. Then we look for vision as we pray. But how do we know it is God who is 'speaking'?

Often, His voice appears as spontaneous thoughts. Sometimes ideas or solutions to problems present themselves. If we have opened ourselves to God's leading, then it is quite reasonable to thank Him for putting such answers into our minds. There is a great danger in over analysing these matters. I take a simple approach. I ask God for direction and that He will keep the thoughts of the enemy away. Then I go with what I believe He is saying. Provided that such inclinations are biblical, then I am happy to move on.

Finally, 'two-way' journaling can help not only record our conversation with God but also facilitate a deepening of our understanding. For some years, I have written what I sensed God was speaking to me. It is like dictation. He speaks and we respond. And having a record is helpful as we move forward.

STEWARDING GOD'S WORDS

What we write or record as audio or video, we may later review. We 'steward well' the revelation that God has given us when we consider it again. Stewarding well, or being responsible for what God says to us, is so important. At the very least, it helps us remember when we can be prone to forget. But more than that, this reinforces the impact of the voice of God so that we remember what He has said.

Suppose that you are asking for direction in a particular matter. It has troubled you for some time and now you sense God has spoken. As you write or record what He has said, you can review and replay these words, underlining their significance. If you return to a place of doubt, you also have revelation from God, which you can revisit. It is easy to lose sight of God's call. But as my late father-in-law often said,

> "Don't doubt in the dark what God has said in the light."

> — STEVE RICHARDS

Our memories are fickle at the best of times. If God has said it, write it down. Review it. This is the language and communication of the Spirit.

8

THE WORD OF GOD

The Bible is amazing! It is a gift from God, and we should treasure it, read it, and apply it. But how do we understand it?

WHAT IS THE WORD?

Wayne Grudem helpfully outlines some different uses of the Word of God in the Bible.[1] As the following Scriptures indicate, these uses are quite varied.

The Word of God can refer to the person of Jesus

> *He is clothed in a robe dipped in blood, and the name by which he is called is **The Word of God**.* (Revelation 19:13)

> *In the beginning was the **Word**, and the **Word** was with God, and the **Word** was God.* (John 1:1)

We use a similar technique when we refer to a person by their title or role. In these examples, 'Word' not only translates a particular Greek word with significance in the first century, but also helps us realise that God is communicating with us through His Son.

The Word of God may be speech by God

(a) God's decrees

> And God **said**, *"Let there be light," and there was light.*
> (Genesis 1:3)

> **By the word of the** Lord *the heavens were made, and by the*
> *breath of his mouth all their host.* (Psalm 33:6)

Here God speaks out a decree. It is powerfully creative.

(b) God's words of personal address

> And the Lord *God commanded the man,* **saying**, *"You may*
> *surely eat of every tree of the garden, but of the tree of the*
> *knowledge of good and evil you shall not eat, for in the day*
> *that you eat of it you shall surely die."* (Genesis 2:16-17)

God also uses speech to communicate with Adam. The man is
able to understand what God is saying and assume responsibility
for disobeying the clear command

God's words are sometimes speech by people

> I will raise up for them a prophet like you from among their
> brothers. And **I will put my words in his mouth**, and he
> shall speak to them all that I command him. And whoever
> will not listen to my words that **he shall speak in my**
> **name**, I myself will require it of him. But the prophet who
> presumes to speak a word in my name that I have not
> commanded him to speak, or who speaks in the name of other
> gods, that same prophet shall die. (Deuteronomy 18:18-20)

> Then the Lord put out his hand and touched my mouth. And the
> Lord said to me, "Behold, **I have put my words in your**
> **mouth**". (Jeremiah 1:9)

Here God communicates His words to humankind *through* other people.

God's words can also be written form

> And he gave to Moses, when he had finished speaking with him on Mount Sinai, the two tablets of the testimony, tablets of stone, **written with the finger of God**. (Exodus 31:18)

> Then Moses wrote **this law** and gave it to the priests, the sons of Levi, who carried the ark of the covenant of the LORD, and to all the elders of Israel ... When Moses had finished writing **the words of this law** in a book to the very end ... (Deuteronomy 31:9, 24)

> And Joshua wrote **these words** in the Book of the Law of God. And he took a large stone and set it up there under the terebinth that was by the sanctuary of the LORD ... (Joshua 24:26)

> If anyone thinks that he is a prophet, or spiritual, he should acknowledge that **the things I am writing to you** are a command of the Lord. (1 Corinthians 14:37)

Perhaps this is the most obvious use of 'Word' when it comes to God speaking to us, but as we have seen, it is only one aspect of His communication. God speaks in different ways through the Bible. We can hear His words both directly and indirectly through others.

CHARACTERISTICS OF SCRIPTURE.

What is the Bible all about? First, there is the question of authority —is it God's word? It claims to be as the following examples illustrate:

> *All Scripture is breathed out by God and profitable for teaching, for reproof, for correction, and for training in righteousness* (2 Timothy 3:16—referring to the OLD TESTAMENT at least)

> *And count the patience of our Lord as salvation, just as our beloved brother Paul also wrote to you according to the wisdom given him, as he does in all his letters when he speaks in them of these matters. There are some things in them that are hard to understand, which the ignorant and unstable twist to their own destruction, as they do **the other Scriptures**.* (2 Peter 3:15-16)

> Paul in 1 Timothy 5:18 (*For the **Scripture** says, "You shall not muzzle an ox when it treads out the grain", and, "The labourer deserves his wages."*) quoting Jesus in Luke 10:7 (*And remain in the same house, eating and drinking what they provide, for the labourer deserves his wages. Do not go from house to house.*)

What about clarity—who can understand it? For most of us, we enjoy reading the Bible in our native language. We can all benefit from reading or listening to Scripture. There are still parts that are harder to grasp and these require a little digging or background reading. Sometimes a study Bible will help or a trusted Bible teacher. Ancient habits from elsewhere in the world are not always clear to us today. Nevertheless, read your Bible! Ask God to make His word come alive to you, give you insight and understanding, and change the way you live.

Then there is the question of sufficiency—do we need more? What about prophecy? How do we balance the written and spoken 'now word' of God? We recognise our Father speaks to us in various ways. In a previous chapter, we touched on His influence on our thoughts. He also communicates through the Bible, what we see around us, and prophetic statements. God will never contradict Himself. A prophetic word that relates to a particular issue we are facing will always be consistent with the Bible.

Therefore, knowing what God has revealed in Scripture is essential. We must be readers and students of the Bible without it ever becoming an academic exercise.

Necessity—can you live without it? You may survive, but you will never thrive if the Bible is not part of your everyday experience. We need that constant, reliable input. And so here is a challenge: read, listen (or both) to a passage of Scripture every day and watch God change your life one step at a time.

CHALLENGE

I attribute this statement to Joel Osteen and his late father, John. Regardless of any controversies relating to that ministry, the words that follow have the power to transform our lives if we let them:

> "This is my Bible. I am what it says I am. I have what it says I have. I can do what it says I can do. Today, I will be taught the Word of God. I boldly confess: My mind is alert, my heart is receptive. I will never be the same.
>
> I am about to receive the incorruptible, indestructible, ever-living seed of the Word of God. I will never be the same. Never, never, never. I will never be the same. In Jesus' name. Amen."

Let's read and be changed. When we ignore the written Word of God we refuse to access God's provision for His people. It is as simple as that.

9

JESUS OUR MODEL

To whom do we look for our inspiration?

THE LIFE OF JESUS

The devotional *My Utmost for His Highest* has remained relevant for about 100 years, as this reading demonstrates:[1]

> Joy comes from seeing the complete fulfilment of the specific purpose for which I was created and born again, not from successfully doing something of my own choosing. The joy our Lord experienced came from doing what the Father sent Him to do. And He says to us "Peace be with you. As the Father has sent me, I also send you." (John 20:21)
>
> — OSWALD CHAMBERS

Intimacy, peace, service, power and authority, and understanding characterise this remarkable life, and we will touch on each of these.

First, Jesus models intimacy with the Father.

> *Very early in the morning, while it was still dark, Jesus got up, left the house and went off to a solitary place, where he prayed.* (Mark 1:35[2])

Jesus finds His nourishment in doing His Father's will:

> *"My food," said Jesus, "is to do the will of him who sent me and to finish his work"* (John 4:34)

just as our heart's desires flow from delight in God:

> *Delight yourself in the* LORD *and he will give you the desires of your heart.* (Psalm 37:4)

Intimacy keeps our vision, enthusiasm, and interest alive. It enables us to live an undefeated life and to persevere. It keeps us awake and alert.

Second, peace is a hallmark of Jesus' life. He carries peace, and He releases it to others. It is important to Jesus that He guards His peace with His Father and we need to protect the peace within us. It can remain through the storms of life (Mark 4:35-41) and when it characterises our walk with God we can demonstrate extraordinary faith. We declare the truth of the Bible even when the opposite appears to be true.

For example, when all around us is descending into chaos and it is hard to make sense of everything, we can declare that 'in Christ, all things hold together', based on Colossians 1:17. Such a life of peace leads to deep-rooted joy and is truly attractive.

Third, Jesus lives a life of service (Mark 10:45). We, too, are here for others. This is a countercultural way to live. Service and compassion link closely together, and lead to miracles of healing and provision.[3] And the ultimate act of service is the washing of the disciples' feet, including those of Judas (John 13:1-17).

Fourth, Jesus demonstrates a life of power and authority. This is completely compatible with peace and service. When we follow His example of breaking strongholds, we bring a genuine revelation of Jesus Christ to our world. We come into agreement with what God is saying:

> ... *on earth as it is in heaven.* (Matthew 6:10)

Finally, Jesus understands the danger of temptation. It is easy to question God (Genesis 3:1-7). However, we can have confidence in what He is saying and reveals to us. Questioning our identity is also common. This is the challenge that Jesus meets in the wilderness (Matthew 4:1-11). But when we know who we are in Christ, the enemy is no match for us. We understand that our abilities, roles, and titles do not define us. God's view is the only one that matters. He has redeemed us (Galatians 3:13), He has made us rich (2 Corinthians 8:9) and we are in Christ (1 Corinthians 1:30).

Looking back may be disheartening, but this is how Paul encourages the Philippian believers:

> *I want to know Christ and the power of his resurrection and the fellowship of sharing in his sufferings, becoming like him in his death, and so, somehow, to attain to the resurrection from the dead. Not that I have already been made perfect, but I press on to take hold of that for which Christ Jesus took hold of me. Brothers and sisters, I do not consider myself yet to have taken hold of it. But one thing I do: Forgetting what is behind and straining towards what is ahead, I press on towards the goal to win the press for which God has called me heavenward in Christ Jesus.* (Philippians 3:10-14)

GETTING BACK TO JESUS

We get caught up with so much in our lives and this is often no less true of Jesus-followers. So make this commitment as you go forward: with God's grace, simply follow Him. Discipleship has always been about following Jesus. It still is. And it always will be. Everything else is ornamental.

10

THE FATHER HEART OF GOD

One of the most important keys to unlocking our spiritual identity is to understand God's Father heart. If our experience of an earthly father is negative, this can easily influence our view of God. You may have had an absent father, one who was physically present but emotionally absent, or abusive. These traumas are real and can have lasting impact (see the chapters on Inner Healing below).

First, what does the Bible say about God's Father role? Scripture speaks powerfully for itself. Resist the temptation to ignore or skim over these passages.

GOD...

... the creator:

> Yet you, LORD, are our Father. We are the clay, you are the potter; we are all the work of your hand. (Isaiah 64:8)

... the provider:

> If you, then, though you are evil, know how to give good gifts to

your children, how much more will your Father in heaven
give good gifts to those who ask him! (Matthew 7:11)

… the friend and counsellor:

For to us a child is born, to us a son is given, and the government
will be on his shoulders. And he will be called Wonderful
Counsellor, Mighty God, Everlasting Father, Prince of Peace.
(Isaiah 9:6)

… the corrector:

And have you completely forgotten this word of encouragement
that addresses you as a father addresses his son? It says, "My
son, do not make light of the Lord's discipline, and do not lose
heart when he rebukes you, because the Lord disciplines the
one he loves, and he chastens everyone he accepts as his son."
Endure hardship as discipline; God is treating you as his
children. For what children are not disciplined by their
father? If you are not disciplined—and everyone undergoes
discipline—then you are not legitimate, not true sons and
daughters at all. Moreover, we have all had human fathers
who disciplined us, and we respected them for it. How much
more should we submit to the Father of spirits and live! They
disciplined us for a little while as they thought best; but God
disciplines us for our good, in order that we may share in his
holiness. No discipline seems pleasant at the time, but
painful. Later on, however, it produces a harvest of
righteousness and peace for those who have been trained by it.
(Hebrews 12:5-11)

… the redeemer:

The LORD is compassionate and gracious, slow to anger,
abounding in love. He will not always accuse, nor will he

harbour his anger forever; he does not treat us as our sins deserve or repay us according to our iniquities. For as high as the heavens are above the earth, so great is his love for those who fear him; as far as the East is from the West, so far has he removed our transgressions from us. (Psalm 103:8-12)

… the comforter:

Praise be to the God and Father of our Lord Jesus Christ, the Father of compassion and the God of all comfort, who comforts us in all our troubles, so that we can comfort those in any trouble with the comfort we ourselves receive from God. (2 Corinthians 1:3-4)

…the defender and deliverer:

Whoever dwells in the shelter of the Most High will rest in the shadow of the Almighty. I will say of the LORD, "He is my refuge and my fortress, my God, in whom I trust." (Psalm 91:1-2)

… the Father:

"I will be a Father to you, and you will be my sons and daughters, says the Lord Almighty." (2 Corinthians 6:18, quoting 2 Samuel 7:14)

… the father who loves:

[Jesus said,] the Father himself loves you because you have loved me and have believed that I came from God. (John 16:27)

… the father of the fatherless:

*A father to the fatherless, a defender of widows, is God in his holy
    dwelling.* (Psalm 68:5)

Embrace these aspects of God's Father heart. Such passages speak
volumes about the God which we serve. They give us fresh understanding and appreciation of all that He is prepared to be and to
do. What a motivation for every Jesus-follower to reflect the
Father heart to an orphaned world.

THE 'PRODIGAL FATHER' IN LUKE 15:11-32

Read this familiar passage and focus on the actions of the father.
Note how he embraces the son, intimately accepts him and
restores him. What is God speaking to you about His response to
your actions? It may help to read the account in a different Bible
translation. Be open to seeing the Father differently.

If you are very familiar with this passage, ask God to give you
eyes to see, ears to hear and a heart to understand. Only then can
we carry His message to those who so desperately need God's
healing and restorative touch.

OUR CHALLENGE

Our society influences our beliefs and behaviour more than we
realise. It programmes us to note what we lack and then look at
what we can buy to make up for it! Or perhaps, thinking that
others have it better than us, we are tempted to change career or
location. We then import this perspective into our walk with God
and focus on our deficiencies. This cripples our walk with Him
and makes us ineffective witnesses to His grace.

Whilst we all acknowledge that there is much yet to learn and put
into practice, and the Bible emphasises this, it is also true that God
reminds us of who we are. This is His starting point. From there,
we can move forward with confidence and humility.

Fear always tells you what you're not, what you don't have, what you can't do and what you'll never be. The Father always tells you who you really are, what He's given you, what Christ has already done for you, and all that *shall be* in your future.

— DUANE WHITE

This is a great reminder.

11

LIVING AS SONS AND NOT ORPHANS

Once we begin to appreciate the Father heart of God, we realise that we are His children.

> *"How great is the love the Father has lavished on us, that we should be called children of God! And that is what we are! The reason the world does not know us is that it did not know him. Dear friends, now we are children of God, and what we will be has not yet been made known. But we know that when he appears we shall be like him, for we shall see him as he is."* (1 John 3:1-2)

Jesus talked about the love of God based on intense personal experience with His Father, who wants us to see ourselves how He sees us.

KNOW WHO YOU ARE

We believe ourselves more than any other person. The words we speak are very important. They will shape and mould us. If you have ever wondered about your true identity, read this list:[1]

- We are children of God (Romans 8:14-15; Galatians 3:26; 4:6; John 1:12)
- We are saints and no longer sinners (Ephesians 1:1; 1 Corinthians 1:2; Colossians 1:2)
- We are a new creation in Christ; old things have passed away and all things have become new (2 Corinthians 5:17)
- We are in Christ (Ephesians 1:1-4; Galatians 3:26-28)
- We are reconciled to God and are ambassadors of reconciliation for Him (2 Corinthians 5:18-21)
- We are God's workmanship, created in Christ for good works (Ephesians 2:10)
- We are citizens of Heaven (Ephesians 2:19; Philippians 3:20)
- We are members of Christ's body (1 Corinthians 12:27)
- We are united with the Lord and one spirit with Him (1 Corinthians 6:17)
- We are the temple of the Holy Spirit (1 Corinthians 3:16; 6:19)
- We are a friend of Christ (John 15:15)
- We are slaves of righteousness (Romans 6:18)
- We are chosen and anointed by Christ to bear fruit (John 15:16)
- We are righteous and holy (Ephesians 4:24)
- We are hidden with Christ in God (Colossians 3:3)
- We are the salt of the earth (Matthew 5:13)
- We are the light of the world (Matthew 5:14)
- We are an expression of the life of Christ and we will share in His glory (Colossians 3:4)
- We are chosen of God, holy and dearly loved (Colossians 3:12; 1 Thessalonians 1:4)
- We are children of light (1 Thessalonians 5:5)
- We are more than conquerors through Christ (Romans 8:37)
- We are God's living stones, being built up in Christ as a spiritual house (1 Peter 2:5)

- We are a chosen generation, a royal priesthood, a holy nation (1 Peter 2:9)
- We are strangers to this world (1 Peter 2:11)
- We are children of God who always triumph in Christ and release His fragrance in every place (2 Corinthians 2:14)
- We are seated in Heavenly places in Christ (Ephesians 2:6)
- We are redeemed by the blood of the Lamb (Revelation 5:9)
- We are part of the bride of Christ and making ourselves ready for Him (Revelation 19:7)
- We are true worshippers who worship the Father in spirit and truth (John 4:24)

These truths are remarkable. God knows who we are. We can trust Him.

THE FATHER DELIGHTS IN US AND WANTS US TO WALK IN OUR SONSHIP

Read Eugene Peterson's paraphrase from part of Ephesians 1:

*How blessed is God! And what a blessing he is! He's the Father of our Master, Jesus Christ, and takes us to the high places of blessing in him. Long before he laid down earth's foundations, he had us in mind, had settled on us as the focus of his love, to be made whole and holy by his love. Long, long ago he decided to **adopt us into his family** through Jesus Christ. (What pleasure he took in planning this!) He wanted us to enter into the celebration of his lavish gift-giving by the hand of his beloved Son. Because of the sacrifice of the Messiah, his blood poured out on the altar of the Cross, we're a free people —free of penalties and punishments chalked up by all our misdeeds. And not just barely free, either. Abundantly free! He thought of everything, provided for everything we could possibly need, letting us in on the plans he took such delight*

> *in making. He set it all out before us in Christ, a long-range plan in which everything would be brought together and summed up in him, everything in deepest heaven, everything on planet earth. It's in Christ that we find out who we are and what we are living for. Long before we first heard of Christ and got our hopes up, he had his eye on us, had designs on us for glorious living, part of the overall purpose he is working out in everything and everyone. It's in Christ that you, once you heard the truth and believed it (this Message of salvation), found yourselves home free—signed, sealed, and delivered by the Holy Spirit. This signet from God is the first instalment on what's coming, a reminder that we'll get everything God has planned for us, a praising and glorious life.* (Ephesians 1:3-14 MSG)

Such 'glorious living' is our inheritance. The best use of our time is to read the words of Scripture and let them wash over us. What else can we learn?

ROYAL PRIESTHOOD

> *But you are a chosen people, a royal priesthood, a holy nation, a people belonging to God, that you may declare the praises of him who called you out of darkness into his wonderful light.* (1 Peter 2:9)

Of course, this is true in a collective sense—the church—rather than an individual sense. But equally, what is true corporately for a people, priesthood and nation is also the case for each of us: a chosen person, a royal priest and a holy citizen. Once we grasp this, our perspective radically changes.

Our identity then affects our behaviour:

- Since we are not under the law, we do not need to strive to earn God's favour. He wants us to enter His rest;
- Because we are dead to sin and alive in Christ, we live from a place of empowered grace;
- As we have the mind of Christ (1 Corinthians 2:16), we think like Him and not like the world; we practice Kingdom thinking; we walk to the heartbeat of Heaven, releasing God's kingdom wherever we go.

How much of God's perspective has become our own? Or do we have so much from our past that blinds us to our position in Christ? Are we unable to see life from a heavenly viewpoint? This is a serious challenge that we must face with integrity and the willingness to move forward. Many followers of Jesus stagnate in their spiritual growth and suffer from life-restricting anxiety. This does not have to be.

FATHER AND CHILDREN

We can enjoy a childlike relationship with our heavenly Father. He has demonstrated His unconditional love and we can live as recipients of all that He has provided for His children. Walk with Him as His child, and not as an orphan. Enjoy His pleasure. Know your identity as a prince or princess in His Kingdom.

INNER HEALING: BACKGROUND

We are confident in approaching God for His intervention in our lives because of our relationship with Him. When we receive the revelation of His father's heart, we know He will walk with us in all that we face and bring both physical and inner healing.

HOW TO UNDERSTAND OUR COVENANTAL GOD

Inner healing is possible when we appreciate God keeps His promises. He is a covenantal God. Although that word appears outdated, it describes a wonderful commitment between God and those He created.

Deuteronomy 4:13 describes the 10 commandments as God's covenant, and then Deuteronomy 28:1-14 lists all the blessings available to those who choose to obey God's commandments. Scripture shows us He can never break His covenant:

> *God is not human, that he should lie, not a human being, that he should change his mind.* (Numbers 23:19a)

> *If we are faithless, he remains faithful, for he cannot disown himself.* (2 Timothy 2:13)

A covenant is an agreement between two or more parties. A simple example of a contractual agreement is purchasing an item in a shop. We agree to pay the price required, and the shop agrees to supply the goods.

We can choose to break our covenant with God. However, as we have seen, He is incapable of breaking His covenant because doing so would be contrary to His nature. He cannot be untrue to Himself.

Adam broke the first covenant between God and humanity (Hosea 6:7). The intimacy promised by God in the Garden of Eden depends on obedience:

> You must not eat from the tree of the knowledge of good and evil,
>   for when you eat of it, you will surely die. (Genesis 2:17)

When Adam and Eve listen to the serpent (Genesis 3:1), they allow themselves to doubt God's character. After breaking their covenant with God, they step outside His protection. Spiritual death begins at that moment. The enemy receives the authority designed for humankind and keeps it until Jesus defeats him at the cross.

Through Jesus, God establishes a new covenant with humanity. Jesus lives, fulfils the law, dies, rises again, and breaks the curse of the law of sin and death. He takes back the keys of authority that the enemy stole. Jesus establishes Kingdom authority for His people so that even in this fallen world, we can exercise God's authority over the powers of the enemy.

As a Jesus-follower you can declare these words with confidence:

Because of God's amazing love and the obedience of Jesus Christ, I am powerful and have authority over sin and darkness. I do not need to fear or yield to sin. I walk in God's Kingdom authority. Nothing can take this from me unless I choose to partner with anything contrary to God's nature.

Since God created us in His image,[1] we need to understand the nature of humanity and his intended relationship with Father God. There is a parallel that we may often overlook. God is three in one—Father, Son and Holy Spirit. We also are tripartite—body, soul and spirit. We will look at each of these. First, let us consider the body.

BODY

> *In the beginning, God created ...* (Genesis 1:1)

Our bodies speak volumes about the wonder of God's creative power. Because of the fall, we are subject to sickness, disease, malfunction, and malformation. We need healing. But even with its many limitations, the body enables us to come in contact with the material world in which we live.

The positive impacts of healthy living are self-evident in our bodies. However, we frequently overlook the benefits to our soul and spirit that result from treating our bodies well. I frequently remind myself of Elijah, whose physical, emotional and spiritual problems were in large part resolved through food and rest (see 1 Kings 19:1-8).

The body is the easiest part of our three-in-one nature to understand. Each of our five senses can be used to experience a physical form. It is when we consider the non-physical that confusion frequently occurs.

SPIRIT

Jesus told the woman at the well,

> *"God is Spirit, and those who worship Him must worship in spirit and truth."* (John 4:24)

Our spirit makes it possible for us to connect with God.

> The spirit is that part by which we commune with God and by
> which we are able to apprehend and worship Him.[2]
>
> — WATCHMAN NEE

This relationship is life-changing:

> *May God himself, the God of Peace, sanctify you through and*
> *through. May your whole spirit, soul, and body be kept*
> *blameless at the coming of our Lord Jesus Christ. The one*
> *who calls you is faithful and He will do it.* (1 Thessalonians
> 5:23-24)

What God has started, He will complete (Philippians 1:6).
However, because of the fall, we can be less than whole in one or
more of spirit, soul and body. When our spirit is out of harmony
with God, who is Spirit, the consequences can be psychological or
physical manifestations. Outside of Christ, our spirit is dead to
God (Ephesians 2:1).

We must let God do the work of inner healing. Remember, the
greatest gift we can offer someone is to help them connect
with Him.

> *[Jesus said] "Come to me, all you who are weary and burdened,*
> *and I will give you rest. Take my yoke upon you and learn*
> *from me, for I am gentle and humble in heart, and you will*
> *find rest for your souls. For my yoke is easy and my burden is*
> *light."* (Matthew 11:28)

SOUL

The soul is the eternal part of our body. It connects us with our
internal world and has three principal dimensions: mind,

emotions, will. The soul acts as a mediator between the body and spirit, and mediates between the spiritual realm (spiritual discernment and faith) and the physical realm (interpreting information from the five senses). This is why the health of our soul is so important.

As Margaret Nagib summarises,[3]

> God dwells in the spirit. Self dwells in the soul. Senses dwell in the body.

Let us consider mind, emotions, and will, in a little more detail.

Mind

The mind processes all incoming information through the physical senses. It thinks and provides the ability to make day-to-day decisions. The mind is not the brain. The brain functions like a computer that stores information and can carry out routine functions that control the body without the mind having to think about what needs to be done next. It is the mind which controls the brain. It can override some of the brain's instructions, for example, such as holding our breath.

Like the body, the mind can be sick, too. Sometimes the presenting issue and the root cause of someone's condition can be very different. Often, people know what they want God to do when seeking healing, but we need to surrender to God's agenda for the person. I remember praying for someone who had a physical problem, and the Lord prompted me to pray about emotional trauma. That was the actual issue.

In Luke 13:10-17, Jesus heals the crippled woman's soul and her body. He sends a powerful message to the surrounding community. She is special and valuable. She is important and deserves to be delivered, free, and whole. He restores her identity and called her 'daughter of Abraham'.[4]

Emotions

Emotions are feelings we experience internally in response to what is happening externally, such as hurt, confusion, turmoil, joy, peace, love, and so on. We experience the best emotions when our spirit, soul, and body are working in perfect harmony and in relationship with God.

There are many sources of emotional pain, including abuse, violence, and damaged emotional responses.

Humanity has become expert at putting on a mask and hiding genuine feelings. Emotions can be sick and need healing. God can do it. Jesus' death and resurrection are about more than our eternal destiny. They provide a full life we can enjoy now.

Will

This is the part of the soul with which we decide how to love. Jesus said to His disciples,

> *"Watch and pray so that you will not fall into temptation. The spirit is willing, but the flesh is weak."* (Matthew 26:41)

The enemy wants our wills to be subject to our flesh instead of the other way around. A person who walks in wholeness and obedience before God is one whose will is under the Lordship of Christ and whose flesh life is under His control. Crucifying our flesh is not a popular message, but it is the road to wholeness (holiness).

Many are so sick in this area that they are incapable of making the right choices. However, healing is possible. Often it will involve deliverance because we have permitted the enemy to control certain areas. To remain free, the person will need to continue to walk in obedience under the Lordship of Christ.

POTENTIAL CONFUSION

First, a note about the English word 'heart'. This is an inconsistent translation of the Hebrew *lev/levav* and the Greek *kardia*. As a general rule, 'heart' has many similarities with the soul as it is the seat of our emotions, intellect and will.

Second, we must note the distinction between soul and spirit.

> *[The word of God] is sharper than the sharpest two-edged sword, cutting between soul and spirit, between joint and marrow. It exposes our innermost thoughts and desires.* (Hebrews 4:12)

If we do not recognise that our spirit and soul are different, we may fall into condemnation because the enemy will attempt to undermine the security we have in God. When we experience problems in our soul, we may discount the reality of our new life in Christ. Satan loves to confuse us on this issue so that we remain defeated. God can heal our soul and the reality of our spirit-Spirit connection with God is not in doubt.

ALL TOGETHER

Man comprises spirit, soul, and body. The soul comprises mind, emotions, and will. God wants His special creation to be whole, and He created us to be led by His Spirit. In Eden, sin enters the world because the soul dominates the spirit. Adam and Eve follow their will. This results in a fallen world where sickness is common.

When the body rules a person, they are prone to addictions. When the soul rules the person, mood disorders are clear, such as depression, anxiety, intellectualising, perfectionism, distorted thoughts, and the inability to control emotions.

It is possible for a person to be sick in any one area and that can affect other areas too. Someone might have been physically ill for a long time that leads to emotional illness, resulting in a rebellion against God that damages the spirit.

Someone might be sick in spirit because of bitterness and unforgiveness and then become physically unwell. Many people first forgive and then experience physical healing.

When we walk in wholeness, we experience the reality of these verses:

> *Though our bodies are dying, our spirits are being renewed every day. For our present troubles are small and won't last very long. Yet they produce for us a glory that vastly outweighs them and will last forever. So we don't look at the troubles we can see now; rather, we fix our gaze on things that cannot be seen. For the things we see now will soon be gone, but the things we cannot see will last forever.* (NLT 2 Corinthians 4:16b-18)

Jesus perfectly models healing. He comes near to the people. He values them, honours them, touches them and restores them.

By God's Spirit, power, and word

> "... we can minister to the body, soul, and spirit of man ... His Spirit touching our spirit releases life and as our human spirit is activated, we carry His life and release it to those around us. Our human spirit, when connected to God's Spirit, is able to discern heavenly things and access God's perfect wisdom, truth, and knowledge."[5]

> — MARGARET NAGIB

This is the wonderful potential available to us as children of God and demonstrates the importance of first understanding how God has made us. Then, we can release His power to every aspect of those around us.

INNER HEALING: OUTWORKING

Inner healing is often viewed as the poor relation to physical healing. However, it is immensely powerful.

> The work of inner healing is to evangelise the unbelieving hearts of believers. It is the application of the blood and cross and resurrection life of our Lord Jesus Christ to those stubborn dimensions of believers' hearts that have so far refused the redemption [of] their minds and spirits requested when they invited Jesus in.[1]

> — JOHN AND MARK SANDFORD

Now that we have surveyed the background of terms behind the need for inner healing, we consider how we work this out practically.

WHAT DOES INNER HEALING REQUIRE OF US?

We will consider this under four headings. First, we must dig deep and obey Jesus:

> *"So why do you keep calling me 'Lord, Lord!' when you don't do*
> *what I say? I will show you what it's like when someone*
> *comes to me, listens to my teaching, and then follows it. It is*
> *like a person building a house who digs deep and lays the*
> *foundation on solid rock. When the floodwaters rise and break*
> *against that house, it stands firm because it is well built. But*
> *anyone who hears and doesn't obey is like a person who builds*
> *a house without a foundation. When the floods sweep down*
> *against that house, it will collapse into a heap of ruins."*
> (NLT Luke 6:46-49)

What is Jesus calling us to do? The need for physical healing is at least matched by the need for inner healing. Knowing that the old life is dead, we prevent it from springing back into life. In Luke 6, Jesus addresses those who already know Him.

Inner healing, therefore, is the discipline of digging deep under the guidance of the Holy Spirit. There are aspects of the old life that should be dead: lies, roots of bitterness, unforgiveness and so on. We must discover what is trying to spring back to life and take it to the cross, where Jesus can attend to it.

Second, our minds and our hearts must believe the same, we must integrate them. It is possible to know something intellectually but not believe it. Our hearts can so easily refuse the grace of Jesus, and this leads to unbelief.

> *If you declare with your mouth, 'Jesus is Lord,' and believe in*
> *your heart that God raised him from the dead, you will be*
> *saved. For it is with your heart that you believe and are*
> *justified, and it is with your mouth that you profess your*
> *faith and are saved.* (Romans 10:9-10)

Inner healing reaches those parts of the heart that have not embraced the reality of the finished work of Christ. If we only believe in our minds, we will not live out the good news. The Gospel must touch our hearts.

Third, we die to ourselves by inviting Jesus to complete our transformation. He crucifies any desires, thoughts, or emotions that are contrary to His nature. We invite Him to be Lord of our lives. As Paul says,

> *Those who belong to Christ Jesus have nailed the passions and desires of their sinful nature to his cross and crucified them there.* (NLT Galatians 5:24)

Finally, we renew our minds (Romans 12:2). God loves to renew and restore (Isaiah 61). He turns deserts into gardens, weaknesses into strengths, shame into honour, mourning into joy and despair into praise. Transformation means the enemy has lost and Romans 8:28 becomes a reality in the life of God's child:

> *God causes everything to work together for the good of those who love God and are called according to his purpose for them. (NLT)*

Inner healing does not erase a memory or change our personal history. But it enables us to see God's hand at work so we can embrace and cherish even the worst moments of our lives. We see God has written eternal lessons on our hearts and prepared us to minister to others who have suffered similarly.[2] We know He has healed us when we can look back on everything with a grateful heart. This takes time and is a process. Be kind to yourself!

Inner healing transforms our characters to reflect the nature of Christ. We become like Him.

> *[We] speak the truth in love, growing in every way more and more like Christ ...* (NLT Ephesians 4:15).

The aim is to see both individuals, and the entire body of Christ, changed to

> ... *maturity, to the measure of the full stature of Christ.* (NRSV Ephesians 4:13b)

WHAT INNER HEALING DOES NOT DO

It is important that expectations are not raised prematurely or falsely. In such cases, dashed hopes can lead to further problems that will need more help. We do not want people to need inner healing from a bad experience that should have brought life!

First, inner healing does not provide a quick fix for that which is broken. That is like putting a new patch on an old garment. Instead, our former nature has to die. Jesus became death for us and we need to reckon our old self dead on the cross with Christ (Romans 6:11). God replaces our old habits with resurrection life. Jesus said,

> *"I tell you the truth, unless a kernel of wheat is planted in the soil and dies, it remains alone. But its death will produce many new kernels—a plentiful harvest of new lives. Those who love their life in this world will lose it. Those who care nothing for their life in this world will keep it for eternity."* (NLT John 12:24-25)

And so, rather than fixing what is broken, Jesus replaces it with something far better: Himself and His life lived in and through His people.

Second, inner healing is not behaviour modification. It is spiritual transformation. God transforms our hearts so that godly behaviour flows from the finished work of Christ. Life's challenges provide many varied opportunities for this change. This healing is not skin-deep, concerned with only restoring someone's self-image. It introduces people to their new identity in Christ. We did not deserve it or earn it and cannot maintain it. We put our confidence in what the Holy Spirit will do through us. Our strength does not lie in our achievements, but in what Christ is in us.[3] Self-image may give glory to a person; a Christ-centred identity gives glory to God.

Third, inner healing is more than comfort. It is a hope in the power of God to purify and sanctify a person's life. We must be secure in God and His truth and comfortable to let Him work in our lives and the lives of others. His glory is at stake. We should do everything for the honour of His name.

Fourth, inner healing is far more than positive thinking. Healing exchanges truth for the lies we believe and allows God's truth to transform our hearts, our minds, emotions, and behaviour. We become different people. Inner healing does not promise us a smooth ride in life. It takes humility, courage, integrity, persistence, vision, commitment, and faith, to walk out God's transformation. There will be opposition and resistance.

The enemy will attack inner healing because he does not want to see people set free. Our mission is to make disciples by taking up the cross and following Jesus. We carry not only the good news of redemption, but also that of healing and transformation. We must not fear what others may think or say.

HOW DOES INNER HEALING MINISTER?

There is no magic formula. Instead, we prayerfully and compassionately minister to the genuine needs of people just like us. We connect them to God. Often it is appropriate to ask if they need to forgive anyone, since the lack of forgiveness is the root of many problems.

There may be a lie the person is believing that results in turmoil and fear. If we identify this, the person can renounce that lie and repent. They choose to leave that wrong belief behind them and walk instead in the truth of what God has revealed. It may not be obvious that they have believed a lie. In that case, gently lead them in a simple prayer: *Father, is there a lie that I am believing?*

They may have hurt from the past that needs healing. This can be a very sensitive area and so we tread carefully, listening to the prompting of the Holy Spirit. A good prayer is this: *What now?*

As ministers, it is essential that we firmly believe God is a giver of wonderful gifts. When we establish that reality in our thinking, we will convey this confidence to others. We can then encourage them to receive the truth of God's goodness and the freedom that He now grants them. It is time to walk out this freedom, to decide to look forward and to invite God's transforming and sustaining presence into this new season.

It is important to remember that we are loving people back to life. We need God's love and compassion for the person in front of us. Each of us grows and hits plateaus, falls back, surges forward and plateaus again. We need to be patient with ourselves and with one another.

When a person does not really want to come to life, they may direct attack and criticism toward the minister. Be prepared for this. We cannot transform a life; that is God's prerogative. By His grace we can love as He does, otherwise we will wear out and become discouraged.

HEALING BY JESUS

To conclude this chapter, we will consider the man that Jesus heals in John 9. This healing is physical, but several principles relate equally to inner healing. First, read the entire chapter.

The man's blindness is not the result of his sin or that of his parents, despite the Rabbinic statement, there is no death without sin and there is no suffering without iniquity.[4]

— RABBI AMMI

Jesus does not address the cause of the blindness. Instead, He talks about the purpose of his disability. It exists to display the work and power of God in his life. As we minister to people, we may not know the cause of their problem. That is no barrier to God working and setting people free. And it is wise not to speculate about the purpose behind someone's suffering. Leave that to God.

Just as Jesus revealed His Father's mercy and grace, we can do likewise. We too are in a relationship with the Father. Suffering is never pleasant, but Jesus gently heals the man from his blindness. Every aspect of our lives is an opportunity to bring God glory and see His purposes unfold. Suffering is an opportunity to show God's grace. He allows circumstances in our lives that glorify Him by drawing us into deeper intimacy with Himself and revealing His glory.

By healing this blind man, Jesus shows He is the Messiah who brings the new quality of life that the Old Testament prophets promised. We are one with Jesus. He anoints and appoints us to bring a new quality of life to the people we encounter.

Jesus spits on the ground, makes mud with the saliva and spreads the mud over the blind man's eyes. Using saliva for medicinal purposes was common in the ancient world, but people often associated clay with pagan healing. This would have raised questions in the minds of the onlookers.

They probably ridicule and humiliate the blind man for his disability. Spitting in someone's face is an act of humiliation. Jesus takes the shame and curse and turns it into healing. Often, God will use the very things that cause us fear and hurt to heal us.

The man has to go wash in the pool of Siloam. His obedience is a key to his healing. He leaves blind and returns with restored sight. In the same way, after we pray, encourage the recipient to be obedient to the call of God in their life, to walk in faith and to believe that God has done the impossible.

God will work mightily through you as you step out in obedience.

COURAGE

God's people are called to be courageous in a world filled with fear.

DEFINITION OF COURAGE

What does courage mean? Here are some possibilities:

- The quality of mind or spirit that enables a person to face difficulty, danger, pain, etc. without fear.[1]
- Mental or moral strength to venture, persevere, and withstand danger, fear, or difficulty.[2]
- The ability to do something that frightens one.[3]
- Strength in the face of pain or grief.[4]

Synonyms include bravery, pluck, valour, nerve, daring, boldness, backbone, spirit, determination and resolution. We have all witnessed acts of great courage and lived courageous lives ourselves. As followers of Jesus, the Bible reminds us that courage is not only important, but possible.

"Be strong and courageous. Do not be afraid or terrified because

> *of them, for the* Lord *your God goes with you; he will never leave you nor forsake you."* (Deuteronomy 31:6)

> *'This is my command—be strong and courageous! Do not be afraid or discouraged. For the* Lord *your God is with you wherever you go.'* (NLT Joshua 1:9)

> *Be on your guard; stand firm in the faith; be courageous; be strong.* (1 Corinthians 16:13)

But when life gets tough, it is easy to hide away. It is on those occasions that God calls us out of hiding and into a child-like faith in Him. Consider the garden of Eden in Genesis 3:9. Adam and Eve disobey God and hide from His presence. And so God asks,

> *"Where are you?"*

It is not as though He cannot find them; He invites them to reveal themselves, to come out of hiding, to exhibit courage.

SUPERNATURAL COURAGE COMES FROM GOD ALONE

When the apostles encounter opposition they pray and ask the Holy Spirit to empower them to communicate boldly the resurrection power of Christ and to help them stay free from the fear of man.

> *It amazed the members of the council when they saw the boldness of Peter and John, for they could see that they were ordinary men with no special training in the Scriptures. They also recognised them as men who had been with Jesus.* (Acts 4:13)

> *"And now, O Lord, hear their threats, and give us, your servants, great boldness in preaching your word. Stretch out your hand with healing power; may miraculous signs and*

wonders be done through the name of your holy servant Jesus." After this prayer, the meeting place shook, and they were all filled with the Holy Spirit. Then they preached the word of God with boldness. (Acts 4:29-31)

We need to spend time with God to receive His courage. This changes our perspective, and that influences our speech. Consider the twelve spies in Numbers 13-14. Only Joshua and Caleb trust God can work a miracle to defeat overwhelming odds. Their supernatural courage distinguishes them from their fellow spies.

SUPERNATURAL COURAGE REQUIRES US TO THINK LIKE GOD

From Romans 12:1-2, we understand the renewing of our minds transforms us from the inside out. We stop taking our cues from the world and start looking from God's perspective.

The size of human opposition does not impress Him. Consider the examples of Gideon (Judges 6-7) and David (1 Samuel 17).

God shows that there is a solution for every problem, since we have the mind of Christ (1 Corinthians 2:16). Of course, Jesus is the greatest example of someone who thinks like God. He spent time with the Father so that He understood what the Father wanted Him to do and say. Then, when 5,000 needed food (Luke 9), Jesus' intimacy with His Father made the courageous miracle possible.

We abide in His love, fear leaves and courage takes its place.[5] For this to be possible, we must intentionally walk with Jesus and become like Him.

SUPERNATURAL COURAGE INSPIRES PEOPLE

In 1 Samuel 14:1-14, Jonathan and his armour bearer attack a Philistine outpost. It is Jonathan's courage that spills over to his servant. When they defeat the Philistines, the Israelites who have gone over to their enemy's side come out of hiding.

The opposite is also true. When we lose courage, it affects those around us.

> *When Ishbosheth, Saul's son, learns about Abner's death at Hebron, he loses all courage, and all Israel becomes paralysed with fear.* (2 Samuel 4:1).

Remember the courage of those from earlier times. Missionary biographies are very helpful to read. These books influenced me years ago as I learned about William Carey, Hudson Taylor, Amy Carmichael and many more.

SUPERNATURAL COURAGE REQUIRES US TO BE SINGLE-MINDED

We hold on to God's word and meditate on it. We do not walk in our personal authority, but in the name of a greater power. The spirit of the living God lives in us. We are one with Him. He is in us and we are in Him.

David understands how to meditate on God's word. It is something he learned when alone with God, tending his sheep (2 Samuel 7:18-29).

> *Though an army besiege me, my heart will not fear; though war break out against me, even then will I be confident. One thing I ask of the LORD, this is what I seek: that I may dwell in the house of the LORD all the days of my life, to gaze upon the beauty of the LORD and to seek him in his temple.* (Psalm 27:3-4)

Mary, the sister of Martha, knew to focus on the one thing that mattered (Luke 10:38-42), even when every distraction around her screamed *focus on me!*

When we look at Jesus, it does not matter what we face. He refines our hearts and ignites them with the fire of God. But this requires intentionality on our part:

> *Above all else, guard your heart, for everything you do flows from it.* (Proverbs 4:23)

When we go through hard times, we must stand and not allow our circumstances to sabotage our courage. We overcome. We meditate on God's word to receive tenacity and perseverance.

If you feel like giving up, read Paul in 2 Corinthians 11:16-33 and carry on.

> *We faithfully preach the truth. God's power is working in us. We use the weapons of righteousness in the right hand for attack and the left hand for defence.* (2 Corinthians 6:7)

And here are some recent quotations, first from a secular source:

> "When you are going through hell, keep going"
>
> — ATTRIBUTED TO WINSTON CHURCHILL

and then from a stalwart Jesus follower:

> "When a train goes through a tunnel and it gets dark, you don't throw away the ticket and jump off. You sit still and trust the engineer."[6]
>
> — CORRIE TEN BOOM

SUPERNATURAL COURAGE RECOGNISES THAT WE ARE NOT OUR OWN.

Paul tells the Corinthian followers of Jesus,

> *You are not your own; you were bought at a price.* (1 Corinthians 6:19b-20a)

Because God is who He claims, He has a right to our lives. He alone is God. He is *El Elyon*, God Most High (Genesis 4:18), *El Shaddai*, God Almighty (Exodus 6:3) and *I Am* (John 8:58). Jesus, too, proclaims His divinity and His right to rule in our lives. He says,

> *"I am the way, the truth, and the life."* (John 14:6)

He has complete control over our past, present and future, and He gives us all we need. We have no reason to live in fear.

> *For God has not given us a spirit of fear and timidity, but of power, love, and self-discipline.* (2 Timothy 1:7)

> *I also pray that you will understand the incredible greatness of God's power for us who believe him. This is the same mighty power that raised Christ from the dead and seated him in the place of honour at God's right hand in the heavenly realms.* (NLT Ephesians 1:19-20)

Supernatural courage comes when we choose to be "all in" for Jesus. Then, the only thing that matters is that He receives everything that He died for.

REVELATION

We all want to communicate with others, and this requires listening as well as speaking. It is the same when it comes to receiving revelation from God, as we saw in an earlier chapter.[1] But what does this really mean?

DEFINITION

Revelation occurs when something hidden or unclear comes into the open. It can also mean unveiled. Revelation exposes what already exists. Here are some simple examples:

- We pull back the curtain and reveal today's weather;
- He switched on the light and everything became visible;
- A gradual process, like the sun rising.

When we play hide and seek with tiny children, we do not try too hard to hide! We want them to find us. So it is with God, He desires to be found.

> *You will seek me and find me when you seek me with all your heart.* (Jeremiah 29:13)

God has secrets, and He wants to make them known.

> *The secret things belong to the LORD our God, but the things revealed belong to us and to our children forever, that we may follow all the words of this law.* (Deuteronomy 29:29)

When God communicates in this way, we have a responsibility to steward that revelation. In the Old Testament, God reveals Himself to Moses, who does everything the Lord commands. Similarly, we receive revelation when God unveils His secrets so that we can walk in obedience.

David knows the beauty of looking to God:

> *The LORD confides in those who fear him; he makes his covenant known to them. My eyes are ever on the Lord, for only he will release my feet from the snare.* (Psalm 25:14-15)

> *God-friendship is for God-worshippers; they are the ones he confides in. If I keep my eyes on God, I won't trip over my own feet.* (MSG Psalm 25:14-15)

God created us to receive His unveiled secrets in a place of intimacy.

WISDOM AND REVELATION

Paul prayed the Ephesians would experience a spirit of wisdom and revelation.

> *I keep asking that the God of our Lord Jesus Christ, the glorious Father, may give you the Spirit of wisdom and revelation, so that you may know him better.* (Ephesians 1:17)

Why is this important? Revelation brings personal transformation, helping us to identify with Jesus. That can only happen when we 'know him better.'

God's revelation in His Word impacts us through its actions:

> ... *the word of God is alive and active. Sharper than any double-edged sword, it penetrates even to dividing soul and spirit, joints and marrow; it judges the thoughts and attitudes of the heart.* (Hebrews 4:12)

Revelation through the Word of God improves the soil of our lives. It redeems and renews our thinking to reform our reasoning (Romans 12:1-2). It releases hope (Romans 4:17-25) and life.

When the Holy Spirit reveals something to us, we bubble with excitement. Our actions and words are powerful. We depend on God when we realise that without Him, we can do nothing of lasting spiritual significance (John 15:5). In fact, Paul counts everything as rubbish compared to knowing Christ as Lord (Philippians 3:8-9). This is life- and priority-changing.

We handle disappointment maturely when God reveals His character and what He can do. Such wisdom enables us to build on a superior reality:

> *So if you're serious about living this new resurrection life with Christ, act like it. Pursue the things over which Christ presides. Don't shuffle along, eyes to the ground, absorbed with the things right in front of you. Look up and be alert to what is going on around Christ—that's where the action is. See things from his perspective. Your old life is dead. Your new life, which is your real life—even though invisible to spectators—is with Christ in God. He is your life. When Christ (your real life, remember) shows up again on this earth, you'll show up, too—the real you, the glorious you.* (MSG Colossians 3:1-4).

FAITH AND REVIVAL

Revelation requires faith in God. The enemy will challenge any revelation we receive, but we can surrender to God with confidence. He knows what He is doing. Then, others will take note:

- The Israelites understand Moses has been with God (Exodus 3–4)
- The Jewish leaders observe that Peter and John are companions of Jesus (Acts 4:13)

If we live with a fresh revelation from the Holy Spirit, our nation will change. The need is great. But so is God's resource.

What are the implications? God wants to reveal Himself to us. He trusts us with this earth. God placed us here in this season. And so we need a fresh revelation that the same power that raised Jesus from the dead lives in us (Ephesians 1:19b-20). We are in Christ and He is in us, the hope of glory (Colossians 1:27). He designs us to thrive in adversity. We view life through a God-lens and bring changes wherever we go because we have been with Jesus. He calls us to extreme obedience, not to add Him as an optional extra to everything else. He must be at the centre.

We give thanks for those who have gone before us, whose ceiling has become our floor. As we focus on what God is doing and join in with Him, we will witness our families and communities transformed and leave a ceiling on which others can build still further.

If we wish to live from a place of revelation, we must position ourselves to hear from God.

> *I will climb up to my watchtower and stand at my guard post.*
> *There I will wait to see what the Lord says and how he will*
> *answer my complaint.* (Habakkuk 2:1)

Where else would you want to be?

16

GOD'S REST

When we confuse activity with identity, burnout will follow. The driven culture around us influences us more than we realise. It is, therefore, essential that followers of Jesus have a healthy, biblical relationship with rest.

IMPORTANCE OF REST

What does God model for us at the very beginning?

> *On the seventh day, God had finished his work of creation, so he rested from all his work. And God blessed the seventh day ... because it was the day when he rested from all his work of creation.* (NLT Genesis 2:2-3)

> *Remember the Sabbath day ... For in six days, the LORD made the heavens and the earth, the sea, and all that is in them, but he rested on the seventh day. Therefore, the LORD blessed the Sabbath day ...* (Exodus 20:8, 11)

We note God does not rest from tiredness or the inability to continue. Instead, He provides an example of rest and rhythm that He advises us to follow.

Which type of rest is God speaking to you about today? You may rest your body, soul, and spirit. Resting the body is the easiest to understand. After a challenging day, we crave sleep. If rest is elusive, we feel its lack over the next few days. Illness and stress can weary the body, and sometimes the answer is for us to sleep.

Constant availability can lead to mental and physical tiredness. Smartphones are great, but when we allow them to take control, our lives suffer. Consider mealtimes without a phone. It is possible and will add to the meaningfulness of our conversation.

It is essential to restrict work-related online connectivity to avoid burnout. Over the years, I have employed several practices, including:

- Do not check emails before breakfast or just before bed;
- Keep my phone on silent unless an expected call is essential;
- Use apps to restrict software until after a quiet period in the morning or when I have concentrated work periods;
- Remove social media apps from my phone.

You will find what works for you. We are all different and what helps in one season may be unnecessary in another.

Good habits such as these will also benefit our mental rest. Unplugging from constant mental stimulation and problem-solving enables us to recharge. No one can carry on without breaks.

When we rest, we recharge our spiritual batteries, too. Think about your life-affirming, faith-raising intake. Where do you receive spiritual food? To whom do you go, to rediscover God's purposes for your life?

WHAT DOES REST ACCOMPLISH?

God-focused rest resets or recalibrates our fractured lives. Such breaks provide fertile soil for spiritual practices to develop. Tiredness makes everything much less enjoyable. Challenges appear to increase in size, and the temptation to give up becomes overwhelming. These matters are real; we cannot ignore them if we want to live a life of Jesus-honouring discipleship.

When we rest in God, we understand it may be appropriate to say 'no' to requests for our time. We root our identity in Jesus, not our never-ending availability to the needs of others. Of course, when we can, we minister as Jesus taught us. But there are also times when we cannot continue. We can only accomplish what physical and emotional strength will permit. This apparent restriction is a safeguard, as we evaluate calls on our time.

In some seasons, we impose unrealistic expectations on ourselves, which is also dangerous. Our 'need to be needed' alerts us that our identity is no longer based on the words of Jesus. We now crave attention from others.

When rested, we remain calm in a crisis. We maintain a biblical worldview amid unbiblical teaching and practice. We apply the Bible to the challenges we face:

> *A worker who does not need to be ashamed and who correctly handles the word of truth.* (2 Timothy 2:15).

Our rest equips us for future service—we do not 'rest from our work' but 'serve from a place of rest.' This rest is not passive. It is an active pursuit of God that enables His fruit of the Spirit to become a reality, rather than just an aspiration:

> *But the fruit of the Spirit is love, joy, peace, patience, kindness, goodness, faithfulness, gentleness and self-control.*
> (Galatians 5:22-23a)

Consider the life of Elijah in 1 Kings 19:1-8 and how God meets his needs. The prophet's fear is genuine and well-founded. However, exhaustion makes him forget both the power of God and God's ability to sustain Elijah and others.

Look back on seasons when life wore your body or emotions down. Remember how impossible everything appeared. And if that is your current experience, consider changing your daily routine. Get more sleep; eat nutritious food; take regular exercise. And watch God open doors and make rough places smooth.

Godly rest is not laziness, but an acknowledgement that we are not God. Our boundaries and limits are for our protection.

17

CULTURE OF HONOUR

Today, honour is in short supply. It is a sad reality that this is often true in the church, too. Dictionary definitions and synonyms of the word 'honour' vary but will often include: hold in great respect, hold in high esteem, have high regard for, admire, appreciate, value, prize, glory, cherish, revere and worship. Imagine how different our world would be if we found these qualities in greater measure.

GOD'S PERSPECTIVE

The Bible has a lot to say on this topic. Peter encourages his readers:

> For the Lord's sake, submit to all human authority — whether the
> king as head of state, or the officials he has appointed. For the
> king has sent them to punish those who do wrong and to
> honour those who do right. It is God's will that your
> honourable lives should silence those ignorant people who
> make foolish accusations against you. For you are free, yet
> you are God's slaves, so don't use your freedom as an excuse

to do evil. Respect everyone, and love the family of believers.
Fear God, and respect the king. (1 Peter 2:13-17)

Just as we must shape and cultivate culture, we must also be intentional in our approach to honour.

[Honour] is one of the greatest attributes of nobility in the entire Bible. When the kingdom is present inside of us, honourable behaviour comes naturally to us. We give honour to all men not just because they deserve it, but also because we are honourable citizens of the king.[1]

— KRIS VALLOTTON

God models honour for us by sending Jesus:

But when the time had fully come, God sent his Son, born of a
woman, born under law, to redeem those under law, that we
might receive the full rights of sons. (Galatians 4:4-5)

The cross of Jesus shows God's love and honour for us. The cross also shows that Jesus will go to such lengths to honour His Father. We know Jesus does His Father's will. We, therefore, have all the motivation we need to follow the example of Jesus.

We demonstrate honour when we do not treat others as less important than ourselves. This includes respect for those of a different social class or race. We do not act from prejudice, but reflect the love of Jesus.

Honour brings life. Many years before Jesus, Moses speaks the words of God to the Israelites:

Honour your father and your mother, so that you may live long
in the land the LORD *your God is giving you.* (Exodus
20:12)

Honour is an issue of the heart. Paul says to the Colossian believers,

> *Therefore, as God's chosen people, holy and dearly loved, clothe yourselves with compassion, kindness, humility, gentleness and patience. Bear with each other and forgive whatever grievances you may have against one another. Forgive as the Lord forgave you. And over all these virtues, put on love, which binds them all together in perfect unity.* (Colossians 3:12-14)

Honour protects our core values and changes relationships for the better. As we 'come low' to serve and empower others, they succeed (Philippians 2:1-11). As Jesus says,

> *"Whoever wants to be first must be slave of all. For even the Son of Man did not come to be served, but to serve, and to give us life as a ransom for many."* (Mark 10:44-45)

We can call out the greatness in others. In the early days of Israel's monarchy, although Jonathan was King Saul's son, he honoured David:

> *And Jonathan made a covenant with David because he loved him as himself. Jonathan took off the robe he was wearing and gave it to David along with his tunic, an even his sword, his bow and his belt.* (1 Samuel 18:3-4)

Honour is not a matter only of thoughts and words. We must enact it. Jonathan *showed* his love. And so did Jesus:

> *But God demonstrates his own love for us in this: while we were still sinners, Christ died for us.* (Romans 5:8)

Honour is active and leads to transformation, creating environments for growth. It breaks the curse of hopelessness and purposeless living. Paul warned the Romans about divisions between the weak and the strong.

Read this passage and note how Paul brought people together through mutual honour.

> *For we don't live for ourselves or die for ourselves. If we live, it's to honour the Lord. And if we die, it's to honour the Lord. So, whether we live or die, we belong to the Lord. Christ died and rose again for this very purpose—to be Lord both of the living and of the dead. So why do you condemn another believer? Why do you look down on another believer? Remember, we will all stand before the judgment seat of God. For the Scriptures say, "'As surely as I live,' says the Lord, 'every knee will bend to me, and every tongue will declare allegiance to God.'" Yes, each of us will give a personal account to God. So let's stop condemning each other. Decide instead to live in such a way that you will not cause another believer to stumble and fall.* (NLT Romans 14:7-13)

The world often makes a decision about God on the basis of the behaviour of those who claim to follow Him.

18

GIFTING AND CHARACTER

Gifting and character are vital for every follower of Jesus. Contemporary culture frequently overvalues gifting at the expense of anything else. Gifting is God-given and necessary for building the Kingdom. But when our characters are less developed, even the most gifted will falter. The failure may be so stark that anything accomplished previously is overshadowed. We must avoid repeating such tragedies.

We focus on godly gifting throughout much of this book. Now we turn our attention to the quality of a person's life, their character.

CHARACTER TO ACT RIGHTLY

It is not only important to start successfully, but to continue and finish well, walking close to God. The account of King Saul provides sobering reading.

> *Saul waited there seven days for Samuel, as Samuel had instructed him earlier, but Samuel still didn't come. Saul realised that his troops were rapidly slipping away. So he demanded, "Bring me the burnt offering"* ... (NLT 1 Samuel 13:8-9)

Previously (1 Samuel 10:8), the prophet Samuel tells Saul to wait for him at Gilgal, since the new king does not have permission to offer sacrifices. Saul and his men fear the Philistine opposition. And so, with presumption based on impatience, Saul ignores Samuel and begins the sacrifice.

Now he attempts to justify himself.

> *Samuel said, "What is this you have done?" Saul replied, "I saw my men scattering from me, and you didn't arrive when you said you would, and the Philistines are at Michmash, ready for battle. So I said, 'The Philistines are ready to march against us at Gilgal, and I haven't even asked for the LORD's help!' So I felt compelled to offer the burnt offering myself before you came."* (NLT 1 Samuel 13:11-12)

Self-justification is a mark of weak character, and Saul combines that with presumption.

Even then, God, in His grace, gives the Israelites victory in 1 Samuel 14. Now, Saul compounds his problems further by uttering a rash oath:

> *Now the men of Israel were in distress that day because Saul had bound the people under an oath, saying, "Cursed be any man who eats food before evening comes, before I have avenged myself on my enemies!" So none of the troops tasted food.* (1 Samuel 14:24)

As a result, the king's rashness almost results in the execution of his son, Jonathan.

Finally, Saul realises that neither God nor Samuel approves of him. God tells the king to destroy all the spoils from the next campaign, but Saul fails once more. When Samuel challenges the king that he has permitted animals to live,

"It's true that the army spared the best of the sheep, goats, and
*   cattle," Saul admitted. "But they are going to sacrifice them*
*   to the L*ORD *your God. We have destroyed everything else."*
*   (NLT 1 Samuel 15:15)*

We find it easy to rationalise disobedience. Followers of Jesus
must exhibit character to walk a harder path when God requires
them.

CHARACTER TO STAY THE COURSE

Here, Paul is a better example. He encourages the Philippian
believers to keep going.

... I press on to possess that perfection for which Christ Jesus first
*   possessed me. No, dear brothers and sisters, I have not*
*   achieved it, but I focus on this one thing: Forgetting the past*
*   and looking forward to what lies ahead, I press on to reach the*
*   end of the race and receive the heavenly prize for which God,*
*   through Christ Jesus, is calling us.* (NLT Philippians
*   3:12-14)*

Paul faced many challenges, almost certainly resulting in his
death. His encouragement, therefore, carries great weight.

CHARACTER TO MAINTAIN COURAGE

In Acts 4, Peter and John provide leadership to a fledgling church
under persecution. They start boldly, but the Jewish authorities
persecute them.

When [the leaders] saw the courage of Peter and John and
*   realised that they were unschooled, ordinary men, they were*
*   astonished, and they took note that these men had been with*
*   Jesus.* (Acts 4:13)

They pray for more boldness (4:29). And then,

> *After this prayer, the meeting place shook, and they were all filled with the Holy Spirit. Then they preached the word of God with boldness.* (NLT Acts 4:31)

We must move in all that God gives us, but not be surprised if we face opposition. Our God-given courage will sustain us even when other aspects of our lives are in disarray.

CHARACTER TO SERVE

Jesus is the ultimate example here:

> *[Jesus said] "For even the Son of Man came not to be served but to serve, and give his life as a ransom for many".* (Mark 10:45)

Servanthood is the start, the middle, and the end of ministry. No servant is above their master. We must finally grasp the reality that we are all about Jesus, not the other way round.

Jesus is quite blunt about this whilst talking to His disciples, as the following passage not-so-subtly illustrates:

> *"Suppose one of you has a servant ploughing or looking after the sheep. Will he say to the servant when he comes in from the field, 'Come along now and sit down to eat'? Won't he rather say, 'Prepare my supper, get yourself ready and wait on me while I eat and drink; after that you may eat and drink'? Will he thank the servant because he did what he was told to do? So you also, when you have done everything you were told to do, should say, 'We are unworthy servants; we have only done our duty.'"* (Luke 17:7-10)

It is a joy to serve Jesus.

CHARACTER TO DO WHATEVER IT TAKES

There are many contemporary examples of Jesus-followers who have given up everything. All they want is to follow the call of Christ. No sacrifice is too much.

When we follow Jesus wholeheartedly, we develop godly character. Life sometimes throws challenges in our paths that allow us to test the depth of that character. We may find it difficult to submit to authority. But godly leadership is vital, and a character impacted by Jesus will respond well to such spiritual oversight.

When our finances concern us, a godly character can help us avoid reacting from a place of panic, whilst dealing responsibly with what must be resolved.

We often encourage followers of Jesus to show an unoffendable heart and choose not to take offence. We give other people the benefit of the doubt.

TWO LEGS

God has given us two legs to stand on. We need them to be of equal length if we are to stand and walk properly. In the same way, gifting and character are essential. We encourage the development of both so that God's Kingdom grows as we honour Jesus.

What better reason could there be?

GRACE

You may remember being told that grace can be understood as an acronym: **G**od's **r**iches **a**t **C**hrist's **e**xpense. There is truth in this, of course, but the meaning of grace is much broader. First, what does Scripture say?

GRACE IN THE BIBLE

God wants us to understand His amazing grace. Paul writes to the believers in Colosse,

> *... we have heard of your faith in Christ Jesus and of the love you have for all the saints—the faith and love that spring from the hope that is stored up for you in heaven and that you have already heard about in the word of truth, the gospel that has come to you. All over the world, this gospel is bearing fruit and growing, just as it has been doing among you since the day you heard it and understood God's grace in all its truth.*
> (Colossians 1:4-6)

A complete understanding of this grace will take a lifetime. But we can begin our appreciation of grace right now! It helps us live for God. Paul knows his past, but he also recognises how the grace of God has lifted him to a better life.

> *For I am the least of the apostles and do not even deserve to be called an apostle, because I persecuted the church of God. But by the grace of God, I am what I am, and his grace to me was not without effect. No, I worked harder than all of them—yet not I, but the grace of God that was with me.* (1 Corinthians 15:9-10)

Grace strengthens us, which is something that following rules will never do:

> *It is good for our hearts to be strengthened by grace, not by ceremonial foods, which are of no value to those who eat them.* (Hebrews 13:9b)

SO WHAT IS GRACE?

In his 1997 book, *Living in the Grace of God*, Rob Rufus provides nine of what he terms definitions:[1]

Grace is the divine characteristic that enables, furnishes and equips human beings to live in a supernatural dimension.

Grace carries the refreshing reality of God's ongoing acceptance of us–an acceptance not dependent on our failures or successes.

Grace is God's desire to bless us–not [based on] our performance, but [based on] Jesus's performance on our behalf.

Grace rescues us from the syndrome of rejection and insecurity, the tyranny of performance-orientated living and the endless anxiety associated with trying to achieve and earn acceptance by keeping laws and regulations.

Grace reveals that we are loved, valued, and accepted by God as we are. Grace means that God's correction and rebuke do not involve a withdrawal of his acceptance but, rather, ... proof of his love for us.

Grace delivers us from self-effort and the heresy of the self-made person. It is not about what we do for God, but what God does for us.

Grace–true grace–turns disappointment into divine appointment and failure into a stepping stone to success.

Grace brings the sunshine of heaven into our hearts; it releases us from the oppression of people's opinions, ... nullifies Satan's accusations, and ... evaporates guilt and regret.

Grace sets us free to be what God created us to be–an enthusiastic, joyful, spontaneous, unpredictable, risk-taking and secure people.

These examples help us understand grace and its breadth of meaning.

Which one resonates with you? It may provide the release from unrealistic pressure that you crave. We often labour under a burden that God never designed us to carry, such as whether we are worthy of God's grace. Again, Rob Rufus reminds us of the worth of Jesus with a glance into the Old Testament:

The priest did not examine the person who brought the offering— he only examined the lamb… our heavenly Father does not look at us—he looks at the Lamb to see if he is acceptable. And, of course, he is![2]

— ROB RUFUS

John describes Jesus as the Lamb of God (John 1:29), who is completely acceptable to His Father, reminding us that God's grace is complete. Thank you Father!

BITTERNESS

Grace also acts as an antidote to bitterness. Terry Virgo captures this well:

> When you go through hard times, bitterness is waiting at the door, offering you fellowship. 'What a terrible time you've had,' it says. 'How cruel they've been! How unjustly you've been treated.' But bitterness isn't a friendly companion; it's a vile weed [that] puts its roots down deep into people's personalities. Not content to disfigure just one soul, it grows up searching for others who might be willing to draw near. If you yield to its offer of companionship, a root will grow in your soul and you'll defile many others.
>
> The only way to withstand bitterness is to make sure that you don't miss the grace of God. Grace, like an effective weed-killer, can get to the root of bitterness and destroy its power. But you must deliberately obtain grace. You must make a specific choice to refuse bitterness, not once, but many times. Bitterness will repeatedly knock on your door and you must always send grace to answer it.[3]

— TERRY VIRGO

And Paul writes to Titus:

> *For the grace of God that brings salvation has appeared to all men. It teaches us to say "No" to ungodliness and worldly passions, and to live self-controlled, upright and godly lives in this present age, while we wait for the blessed hope—the glorious appearing of our great God and Saviour, Jesus Christ.* (Titus 2:11-13)

Dealing with bitterness is not easy, but it is possible.

THE COMMUNITY OF GRACE

Returning to Rob Rufus and his ninth definition of grace ("grace sets us free to be what God created us to be–an enthusiastic, joyful, spontaneous, unpredictable, risk-taking and secure people"), we realise that grace is not only for individuals. The Bible is clear on this:

> *With great power the apostles continued to testify to the resurrection of the Lord Jesus. And God's grace was so powerfully at work in them all.* (NLT Acts 4:33)

> *Through him and for his name's sake, we received grace and apostleship to call people from among all the Gentiles to the obedience that comes from faith.* (Romans 1:5)

> *But the gift is not like the trespass. For if the many died by the trespass of the one man, how much more did God's grace and the gift that came by the grace of the one man, Jesus Christ, overflow to the many!* (Romans 5:15)

> *And now, brothers, we want you to know about the grace that God has given the Macedonian churches.* (2 Corinthians 8:1)

> *May the grace of the Lord Jesus be with God's holy people.* (NLT Revelation 22:21)

And there are many more examples throughout the Bible, such as the patient father (Luke 15), Noah (Genesis 6–9), Lot (Genesis 18–19; 2 Peter 2:7) and David (2 Samuel 11–12).

Every Jesus follower must increase their understanding of grace. This wonderful gift from God will change our lives.

BIRTHING GOD'S KINGDOM

All that we have considered prepares us to see God's Kingdom come and His will be done where we live, as it is in heaven.

SUPERNATURAL INHERITANCE

Before we can experience the Kingdom of God birthed, we must understand what is ours through what Christ has accomplished. Ephesians 1 is a rich passage and deserves a chapter on its own. For now, however, read these verses and write down what God is highlighting to you.

> *All praise to God, the Father of our Lord Jesus Christ, who has blessed us with every spiritual blessing in the heavenly realms because we are united with Christ. Even before he made the world, God loved us and chose us in Christ to be holy and without fault in his eyes. God decided in advance to adopt us into his own family by bringing us to himself through Jesus Christ. This is what he wanted to do, and it gave him great pleasure. So we praise God for the glorious grace he has poured out on us who belong to his dear Son. He*

is so rich in kindness and grace that he purchased our
freedom with the blood of his Son and forgave our sins. He
has showered his kindness on us, along with all wisdom and
understanding.
God has now revealed to us his mysterious will regarding Christ
—which is to fulfil his own good plan. And this is the plan:
At the right time, he will bring everything together under the
authority of Christ—everything in heaven and on earth.
(NLT Ephesians 1:3-10)

As we understand our identity, we lay a foundation upon which
God will build.

There are considerable kingdom resources available to us:

For this reason, I kneel before the Father, from whom every family
in heaven and on earth derives its name. I pray that out of his
glorious riches, he may strengthen you with power through
his Spirit in your inner being, so that Christ may dwell in
your hearts through faith. And I pray that you, being rooted
and established in love, may have power, together with all the
Lord's holy people, to grasp how wide and long and high and
deep is the love of Christ, and to know this love that surpasses
knowledge – that you may be filled to the measure of all the
fullness of God. (Ephesians 3:14-19)

We access the power of God:

I also pray that you will understand the incredible greatness of
God's power for us who believe him. This is the same mighty
power that raised Christ from the dead and seated him in the
place of honour at God's right hand in the heavenly realms.
(NLT Ephesians 1:19-20)

And we enjoy a demonstrable faith which has intellectual credibility (Ephesians 3:7-13). In Christ, God has given us everything we need.

BIRTHING A MOVE OF GOD

We may feel our hearts will burst if we do not experience God intervene.

> *Oh, that you would burst from the heavens and come down!*
>   (NLT Isaiah 64:1a)

And so, we begin with our personal walk with God. Then we *walk out* what we learn within the context of community. Here are some biblical examples of hungering after God.

- Express desperation for a child (1 Samuel 1). Hannah's focus is on her barrenness, rather than hungering for God. But she went to God in her distress.
- Live a life of prayer (Matthew 6:6-13; Colossians 4:2)
- Learn to surrender (Matthew 6:33; Mark 8:34)
- Learn to persist (Hebrews 12:1-3, 12)
- Understanding God's heart and His ways. Our lives are different. We do not conform to the surrounding culture. (Romans 12:1-2)
- Allow His words to mould and prepare us for what is coming (Matthew 4:4)
- Accept our spiritual authority (Ephesians 2:6, 4:1; 1 Thessalonians 2:12)

Living in a community is the ideal environment to witness a move of God. Consider the following passages. What do they teach us about working together with other Jesus-followers?

- Matthew 28:18-20
- 2 Corinthians 5:14-15
- Galatians 6:2
- 1 Thessalonians 5:11

* * *

I have outlined aspects of our identity in Christ over these previous chapters. Although some areas of identity overlap with our activity, our discussion now shifts gear into other areas of practical Christian ministry.

PART III
OUR ACTIVITY

RESPONDING TO GOD'S CALL

> *"I heard the voice of the LORD saying, 'Whom shall I send? And
> who will go for us?' And I said, 'Here am I. Send me!' He
> said, 'Go ...'"* (Isaiah 6:8-9a)

God is still looking and calling.

LIVE WHOLLY FOR GOD

God wants everything from us. Paul responds to such demands:

> *For I fully expect and hope that I will never be ashamed, but that
> I will continue to be bold for Christ, as I have been in the
> past. And I trust that my life will bring honour to Christ,
> whether I live or die. For to me, living means living for
> Christ, and dying is even better.* (NLT Philippians 1:20-21)

Perhaps the most well known of the five American missionaries
martyred in Ecuador in January 1956 was Jim Elliot. One of his
pithy sayings has challenged followers of Jesus ever since:

He is no fool who gives what he cannot keep to gain what he cannot lose.

— JIM ELLIOT

One of Jim's fellow missionaries was Pete Fleming. His brother later compiled and printed Pete's journal, detailing the group's last contact with the Auca Indians.

Pete's personal journal ends here. Thirty six hours later, an Auca spear pierced his heart and within seconds he was in God's presence. Four years before, Pete had written in his journal, "... I have felt in the last couple days great prayer longings for [the Indians], particularly the Aucas. I do want to be committed to the work there 'laying down my life for their faith.'" [1]

— KEN FLEMING

We root such commitment to the call of God in a clear sense of identity. We must know who we are in Christ and love Him in return:

[Jesus said] "Love the LORD your God with all your heart and with all your soul and with all your mind." (Matthew 22:37, quoting Deuteronomy 6:5)

We 'live out' what God has called us: saint, child of God, hidden in Christ, ambassador of Christ, new creation, righteous, holy, citizen of heaven, God's workmanship, a temple of the Holy Spirit, light of the world, part of the true vine, partaker of a heavenly calling, more than a conqueror, a living stone, a chosen generation, royal priesthood, the devil's enemy, seated in Heavenly places, recipient of every spiritual blessing, redeemed by the blood of the Lamb, the bride of Christ, and a true worshipper who worships in spirit and truth.

Read this list again and reflect on how God sees you.

Living wholly for God is costly but worthwhile:

> *And through your faith, God is protecting you by his power until you receive this salvation, which is ready to be revealed on the last day for all to see. So be truly glad. There is wonderful joy ahead, even though you must endure many trials for a while. These trials will show that your faith is genuine. It is being tested as fire tests and purifies gold—though your faith is far more precious than mere gold. So when your faith remains strong through many trials, it will bring you much praise and glory and honour on the day when Jesus Christ is revealed to the whole world.* (NLT 1 Peter 1:5-7)

We put God first (Matthew 6:33).

BE A HISTORY MAKER AND A WORLD CHANGER

Consider these biblical examples of men and women who lived the life of faith:

- Paul (his Damascus Road experience [Acts 9]; not ashamed of the Gospel [Romans 1:16])
- Abraham (a friend of God and father of the faith. Genesis 12–22)
- David (prepared to be hidden so that God could prepare him to influence and inspire many [1 Samuel 17:34-37])
- Moses (Led the people out of captivity [Exodus 3])
- Jonah (he experienced the God of the second chance [Jonah 3:1])
- Daniel (remained faithful and lived counter-culturally [Daniel 1:8])
- Joshua (led the people into the promised land [Joshua 1])
- Ruth (though she was a Moabitess, she became part of the line of David and then Jesus [Ruth 4:22])

- Esther (in the palace for "such a time as this" to save her people [Esther 4:14])

BE INTELLECTUALLY AND EXPERIENTIALLY CONSISTENT

James is very straight with his readers:

> *Do not merely listen to the word, and so deceive yourselves. Do what it says.* (James 1:22)

We can only respond to God's call when we practise what we preach. What is important to God must become important to us. Theory and practice are both vital.

RESPOND TO THE CALL OF GOD

God does not call the qualified, gifted, and equipped. He calls the surrendered, the humble, the dependent, and then He qualifies them, gifts them and equips them. Our lives are all grace:

> *For God saved us and called us to live a holy life. He did this, not because we deserved it, but because that was his plan from before the beginning of time — to show us his grace through Christ Jesus.* (NLT 2 Timothy 1:9)

Obedience to the call of God will not be easy or always make sense to our world. If we can fully understand what we are doing and accomplish God's mission in our own strength, then perhaps this task is instead a plan of our devising. His call is always demanding. He requires us to put Him first in everything. He will challenge and stretch us like nothing else and our lives will be richer.

Say 'yes' to God!

AUTHORITY AND POWER

These are strong words and need a little explanation.

THE TERMS EXPLAINED

The words power and authority evoke many responses. Through several talks and articles by Bill Johnson and others, I have found the following helpful.

First, our authority comes from the commission God has given us and our identity as followers of Jesus. We are authoritative because of who we are. This is profoundly different from exercising an authoritarian approach, where one person dominates another. Our authority is not over people, but the enemy.

Second, the power we exercise flows from an encounter with God that has impacted us to our core. We do not seek encounters, only to add them to a list of our experiences. Instead, we open ourselves to encountering God in everyday life, proving Him in the mundane and the spectacular. Remember, our first encounter is salvation, but may that not be the last!

FOR A PERIOD, JESUS GIVES BOTH POWER AND AUTHORITY TO THE DISCIPLES

In Luke 9, Jesus gives the new disciples a task:

> *When Jesus had called the Twelve together, he gave them power
> and authority to drive out all demons and to cure diseases,
> and he sent them out to preach the kingdom of God and to
> heal the sick.* (Luke 9:1-2)

This early commission occurs before the death and resurrection of Jesus. At this stage, the understanding of the disciples is limited. Later, the resurrected Jesus appears:

> *[He] breathed on them and said, "Receive the Holy Spirit."* (John
> 20:22)

There is more to come for the followers of Jesus. Before His ascension to heaven, He tells them to wait.

> *"I am going to send you what my Father has promised; but stay
> in the city until you have been clothed with power from on
> high."* (Luke 24:49)

In their earlier ministry, the disciples operated with temporary power and authority because Jesus was with them. After His ascension, they would need something permanent.

AUTHORITY—COMES WITH COMMISSION

The so-called 'Great Commission' of Matthew 28 is a key text.

> *Then Jesus came to [the disciples] and said, "All authority in
> heaven and on earth has been given to me. Therefore go and
> make disciples of all nations ..."* (Matthew 28:18-19)

At the very beginning in the garden of Eden, God gives Adam and Eve authority to rule on His behalf. When they sin, they ignore God. They abdicate their authority to the enemy, who misuses it until the time of Jesus. At the cross, Jesus reclaims all authority.

> *You were dead because of your sins and because your sinful nature was not yet cut away. Then God made you alive with Christ, for he forgave all our sins. He cancelled the record of the charges against us and took it away by nailing it to the cross. In this way, he disarmed the spiritual rulers and authorities. He shamed them publicly by his victory over them on the cross.* (NLT Colossians 2:13-15)

Therefore, Jesus is qualified to return the authority to us. We, like Adam and Eve, receive delegated authority from God to act on His behalf.

AUTHORITY ALSO FLOWS FROM IDENTITY

Consider these statements based on Scripture:

- Matthew 28:18-19a *I am a disciple of Jesus*
- Ephesians 1:18-22 *I am a recipient of divine power*
- Ephesians 3:14-20 *I am rooted in love, a recipient of the fullness of God, and a follower of the God of the immeasurably more*
- 2 Corinthians 10:1-5 *I am a spiritual warrior*

When we understand our identity, we live with authority and purpose. We have spiritual muscle, but we must exercise it. That is how our authority grows and we become more effective.

POWER—COMES WITH ENCOUNTER

Jesus says to His disciples,

> *"But you will receive power when the Holy Spirit comes on you,
> and you will be my witnesses ..."* (Acts 1:8)

The disciples are already knowledgeable and experienced. But it is the Holy Spirit encounter that will give them *power*. This is an emotive topic, but one of great importance. Paul reminds the Corinthian believers that the cross of Jesus is a powerful message:

> *For the message of the cross is foolishness to those who are
> perishing, but to us who are being saved, it is the power of
> God.* (1 Corinthians 1:18)

Later, Paul reminds his readers,

> *When I first came to you, dear brothers and sisters, I didn't use
> lofty words and impressive wisdom to tell you God's secret
> plan. For I decided that while I was with you, I would forget
> everything except Jesus Christ, the one who was crucified. I
> came to you in weakness—timid and trembling. And my
> message and my preaching were very plain. Rather than
> using clever and persuasive speeches, I relied only on the
> power of the Holy Spirit. I did this so you would trust not in
> human wisdom but in the power of God.* (NLT 1
> Corinthians 2:1-5)

Only God-given power can make the great difference that our world needs. Such power enables us to love the unlovable with compassion. The Holy Spirit will give us a particular sensitivity to follow His prompting. Sometimes, He releases miraculous abilities that change a person's life forever. Most of all, the power of God enables us to be everything He designed us to be.

WHEN POWER AND AUTHORITY ARE MISUSED

If you have experienced the abuse of someone's power and/or authority, you will need healing. Such misuse is a big concern. Some leaders overstep God-given boundaries, and this results in pain and mistrust. Go to someone you know and with whom you are comfortable. Explain what has happened and ask for prayer support as you work through it all. Be kind to yourself. Take all the time and space you need. Eventually, God will enable you to trust again.

The answer to misuse is healing and a godly appreciation for authority and power in a consecrated life.

A CHALLENGE FOR US ALL

Over 100 years ago, two young men were talking in Ireland. One said, "The world has yet to see what God will do with a man fully consecrated to Him." The other man meditated on that thought for weeks. It so gripped him that one day he exclaimed, "By the Holy Spirit in me I'll be that man." Historians now say that he touched two continents for Christ. His name was Dwight L. Moody.[1]

— BILLY GRAHAM

What about you, and what about me?

BUILDING WITH KINGDOM TOOLS

You may have heard the saying that life is God's gift to us; what we do with that life is our gift to Him. We bear a responsibility to build on the foundations that God has laid:

> *... as fellow citizens with God's people and members of God's household, built on the foundation of the apostles and prophets, with Christ Jesus himself as the chief cornerstone.* (Ephesians 2:19b-20)

LET'S BUILD!

If we want to see the Kingdom of God expand, we must move forward. We build with the tools God has provided. Abiding in Jesus (John 15) is vital, and we work together with others who show equal commitment to the call of God. We move from talking to action:

> *The Kingdom of God is not just a lot of talk; it is living by God's power.* (NLT 1 Corinthians 4:20)

Or, as Eugene Peterson paraphrases this verse,

God's way is not a matter of mere talk; it's an empowered life.
(MSG 1 Corinthians 4:20)

Paul reminds the Roman believers that life comprises more than we sometimes acknowledge:

... the Kingdom of God is not a matter of eating and drinking, but of righteousness, peace, and joy in the Holy Spirit. (Romans 14:17)

To ground ourselves well and position ourselves to move forward, we need to accept the right things about God. A. W. Tozer believed that

What comes into our minds when we think about God is the most important thing about us.[1]

— A. W. TOZER

From a place of intimacy with our Father, we start with our relationship with Him.

There is only one relationship that really matters, and that is your personal relationship to your personal Redeemer and Lord. If you maintain that at all costs, letting everything else go, God will fulfil His purpose through your life. One individual life may be of priceless value to God's purposes, and yours may be that life.[2]

— OSWALD CHAMBERS

Here are some of the Kingdom building tools available to us as followers of Jesus.

THANKSGIVING

A grateful heart transforms us from the inside out. When we rejoice, give thanks to God, and worship, we change our thinking.

> *Worship God if you want the best; worship opens doors to all his goodness.* (MSG Psalm 34:9)

Thanksgiving increases our faith as we remember all that God has done—what He has done before, He can do again. It is hard to overestimate the power of a proper appreciation of God and what He has done.

RIGHTEOUSNESS

Right-living and right-standing before God are vital tools for building His kingdom. Several Scriptures underline the importance of righteousness. Read the following passages and consider how they speak to your current situation.

> *"Blessed are those who hunger and thirst for righteousness, for they will be filled. ... Blessed are the pure in heart, for they will see God."* (Matthew 5:6, 8)

> *For the Scriptures tell us, "Abraham believed God, and God counted him as righteous because of his faith".* (NLT Romans 4:3)

> *... God will also count us as righteous if we believe in him, the one who raised Jesus our Lord from the dead.* (NLT Romans 4:24)

> *For the sin of this one man, Adam, caused death to rule over many. But even greater is God's wonderful grace and his gift of righteousness, for all who receive it will live in triumph*

over sin and death through this one man, Jesus Christ. (NLT Romans 5:17)

Because one person disobeyed God, many became sinners. But because one other person obeyed God, many will be made righteous. (NLT Romans 5:19)

Don't you realise that you become the slave of whatever you choose to obey? You can be a slave to sin, which leads to death, or you can choose to obey God, which leads to righteous living. ... Now you are free from your slavery to sin, and you have become slaves to righteous living. (Romans 6:16-18)

Righteous living is not always easy but it is possible. This lifestyle speaks volumes to the world. People notice how we live, and our right-standing before God strengthens our kingdom building.

PEACE

Jesus is the Prince of peace (Isaiah 9:6). When we live in a close relationship with Him, He is in us, and we are in Him (John 15:4). Remember what Jesus says when He calms the storm in Luke 8:

One day Jesus said to his disciples, "Let us go over to the other side of the lake." So they got into a boat and set out. As they sailed, he fell asleep. A squall came down on the lake so that the boat was being swamped, and they were in great danger. The disciples went and woke him, saying, "Master, Master, we're going to drown!" He got up and rebuked the wind and the raging waters; the storm subsided, and all was calm. "Where is your faith?" he asked his disciples. In fear and amazement, they asked one another, "Who is this? He commands even the winds and the water, and they obey him." (Luke 8:22-25)

The peace that Jesus carries is enough for Him to speak that peace over the elements. What goes on around Him does not define Him. This is such a challenge, particularly if we are easily influenced by our circumstances.

If we lack peace, we can ask God for it. After all, it is a fruit of the Spirit that is the right of every follower of Jesus (Galatians 5:22).

JOY

Circumstances can make us unhappy, but joy shines through even the worst conditions. That is because joy depends on the anticipation and expectation of something wonderful. Joy can focus on a promise or truth and rejoice in anticipation of an eventual breakthrough.

It is a gift from God and a sign that the Holy Spirit is living within us.

> *And the disciples were filled with joy and with the Holy Spirit.*
> (Acts 13:52)

The opposition of the Jews, persecution and expulsion from the area proves that joy is not dependent on circumstances!

Such challenges are frequent in New Testament times.

> *So be truly glad. There is wonderful joy ahead, even though you must endure many trials for a little while. These trials will show that your faith is genuine. It is being tested as fire tests and purifies gold—though your faith is far more precious than mere gold. So when your faith remains strong through many trials, it will bring you much praise and glory and honour on the day when Jesus Christ is revealed to the whole world. You love him even though you have never seen him. Though you do not see him now, you trust him; and you rejoice with a glorious, inexpressible joy.* (NLT 1 Peter 1:6-8)

> *Dear brothers and sisters, when troubles of any kind come your*
> *way, consider it an opportunity for great joy. For you know*
> *that when your faith is tested, your endurance has a chance to*
> *grow. So let it grow, for when your endurance is fully*
> *developed, you will be perfect and complete, needing nothing.*
> (NLT James 1:2-4)

What is true for believers is also true for Jesus.

> *Because of the joy awaiting him, he endured the cross,*
> *disregarding its shame. Now he is seated in the place of*
> *honour beside God's throne. Think of all the hostility he*
> *endured from sinful people; then you won't become weary and*
> *give up.* (NLT Hebrews 12:2b-3)

Remember that superficial happiness may be momentary, but joy can be long-lasting.

LOVE

Unconditional love is fuelled by supernatural power. Perhaps 1 Corinthians 13 is the classic passage on love, but Jesus emphasises it too.

> *"So now I am giving you a new commandment: Love each other.*
> *Just as I have loved you, you should love each other."* (NLT
> John 13:34)

> *"I have loved you even as the Father has loved me. Remain in my*
> *love."* (NLT John 15:9)

Jesus shows unfailing love and faithfulness, frequently moved with compassion for those around Him. Such compassion is sometimes costly, and that can be true for us, too.

Our love for one another will prove to the world that we truly are followers of Jesus (John 13:35). We are compassionate, or merciful, like our Father (Luke 6:36). But first, we must be rooted in the love of God (Colossians 2:7) and clothed in His love (Colossians 3:12-14). This is intensely practical and, at times, challenging. We can ask God for His gift of love—to see the world as He views it—but it is not something we can conjure up or fake. The Bible is very clear about this in Romans 12:9.

> *Don't just pretend to love others. Really love them. Hate what is wrong. Hold tightly to what is good.* (NLT)

> *Love from the centre of who you are; don't fake it. Run for dear life from evil; hold on for dear life to good. Be good friends who love deeply; practice playing second fiddle.* (MSG)

> *Let love be genuine.* (ESV)

The world is hungry and waiting for the real thing. Through our love, we show the love of God. And so, little by little, we build the Kingdom of God.

FIVE FOLD MINISTRY

In many circles, the term five-fold ministry is unknown or unclear. The idea stems from Paul's list in Ephesians 4:

> *It was [Jesus] who gave some to be apostles, some to be prophets, some to be evangelists, and some to be pastors and teachers, to prepare God's people for works of service so that the body of Christ may be built up.* (Ephesians 4:11-12)

Tom Wright gives an alternative emphasis:

> *So these were the gifts that he gave. Some were to be apostles, others prophets, others evangelists, and others pastors and teachers. Their job is to give God's people the equipment they need for their work of service, and so to build up the king's body.* (NTE)

The sentence structure may suggest that pastors and teachers are the same people. In that case, the term 'four-fold' is more accurate, though I will continue to use 'five-fold' throughout this chapter. Either way, there are diverse roles in the church which are necessary to see God's people built up. It is that context that provides the backdrop for the list in verses 11 and 12. Here is a need (spiritual maturity), and this is how we meet that need (five-fold ministry).

MATURITY

We will briefly consider certain aspects of spiritual growth that are vital for the follower of Jesus. We find them in the following verses:

- 4:12 prepared for works of service
- 4:12 build up the body of Christ
- 4:13 reach unity in the faith and our knowledge of Jesus
- 4:13 become mature and genuine, measured by the standard of Christ
- 4:14 no longer acting like infants
- 4:14 no longer influenced by what is around us
- 4:14 no longer subject to the scheming of others
- 4:15 speak the truth in love
- 4:15 grow up in Jesus individually
- 4:16 grow up collectively

We would all agree that these are worthwhile goals.

PRIORITY AND FOUNDATION

Now you together are the Messiah's body, and individually you are members of it. In the church, God has placed apostles first, then prophets, then teachers, then powerful deeds, then gifts of healing, helpful deeds, organisational gifts, different types of languages. (NTE 1 Corinthians 12:27-28)

The apostolic and prophetic ministries play a significant role in the ancient church, which God

... built on the foundation of the apostles and prophets ... (NTE
Ephesians 2:20)

We cannot repeat such foundational tasks. But there remains a
role for apostolic and prophetic people. They build upon what has
gone before, and they also step out to take new ground. They
expand the Kingdom of God.

Controversy and misunderstanding may arise when we apply the
terms apostle and prophet to individuals. Strangely, this is not the
case with evangelists, pastors, or teachers. Perhaps that is because
the church has accepted the latter three throughout much of
history. The first prophets and apostles had a unique role in laying
a foundation for all that followed. However, today there remains a
call to expand the Kingdom of God, and this call requires apostolic and prophetic people.

Therefore, it may be helpful to refer more to apostolic and
prophetic function than the terms apostles and prophets. I appreciate that some may disagree, considering this a watering-down.

What exactly do we mean by the terms apostolic, prophetic, evangelistic, pastoral, and didactic (teaching)?

FUNCTION

It is unfortunate the New Testament does not define these terms.
Ephesians 4 suggests that each role plays a part in building up the
whole body of Christ. We find no place for the promotion of the
individual, since the only context for ministry is the corporate
church and those yet to join us.

Apostolic ministry often focuses on planting a new expression of
the Kingdom, breaking fresh ground and bringing heaven to
earth. Such a person is passionate about creating a new culture.
Kingdom values play a large part in both thinking and practice.
Frequently, an apostolic person considers a local move of God

within the context of a wider area. Paul is a natural example of this work in the New Testament.

Biblical prophetic ministry often involves the practice of speaking God's truth to those in power. Today, this can occur outside the church, when prophetic voices address local or national issues. Within church life, prophecy may speak to leaders or individuals. It has little to do with the valuable and appreciated encouragement often given, particularly to Christians. Both prophecy and encouragement are necessary, but they are not the same.

We appear to better understand evangelistic ministry, though we are in danger of limiting it to certain, well-known forms. The remarkable work of people such as the late Billy Graham has transformed the lives of countless people around the world. Equally, those who share their faith as they share their lives are also engaged in evangelism. The Kingdom call of God is to make disciples, not converts, and so those who profess faith in Jesus must also grow.

Pastoral ministry, or shepherding, accepts people as they are and loves them too much to let them stay that way. There is a coming alongside, navigating well the challenges and milestones of life. This ministry ties in so well with discipleship. We learn from one another as we spend time in each other's company. Listening, advice and journeying together provide fertile soil for personal and corporate walks with God.

The teaching ministry often links to pastoral work but can also stand on its own. Teachers are diligent in their desire to understand and apply the Bible correctly. They do not desire knowledge for its own sake, but want to share their understanding with others. We can only lay Kingdom foundations with an understanding of the word of God.

CHURCH GOVERNMENT

In the main, pastors or teachers led churches, regardless of the denomination. They exhibited a tendency to be inward looking, carefully guarding the truth, but perhaps missing the opportunities for outreach and growth. Of course, this weakness can also occur with other types of leaders!

But what would happen if we also embrace those gifted apostolically, prophetically, and evangelistically? We would fulfil the mission of Jesus for His church: making disciples.

When we consider that every part of God's provision is necessary, we flourish. We need a supernatural engagement with the local and broader scene, hearing the voice of God for our times. Genuine connection with those around us, walking a pilgrim pathway together, makes us more like Jesus.

Ephesians 4 is more important than we realise.

EFFECTIVE PRAYER

The Bible promotes prayer from Genesis to Revelation. The Scriptures contain examples of several specific postures: sitting, standing, kneeling, lying with the face to the ground, and lifting the hands. There are also different kinds of prayer. Consider the following examples:

- the prayer of faith (James 5:15)
- the corporate prayer of agreement (Acts 4:23-31)
- request or petition (Philippians 4:6)
- thanksgiving (Psalm 95:2)
- worship (Acts 13:2-3)
- dedication and submission (Matthew 26:39)
- intercession (1 Timothy 2:1)
- praying in the Spirit (1 Corinthians 14:14-15)

There are different ways to pray the varied types of prayers. What is most important is that we pray!

PRAYER IS AN EXCHANGE

Prayer is a two-way conversation between God and His children. We receive from God as much as we share our hearts and needs with Him. Prayer enables us to understand God, His mind, and His ways.

Although we can come to Him as we are, we receive Him in His perfection. That is quite the exchange!

We need to meet with God regularly if we wish to live our lives in a place of intimacy. We stay connected to the vine that is Jesus (John 15:1-8).

WORDS ARE IMPORTANT

Our choice of language influences how we deal with others (Proverbs 18:21). But with prayer, we take it a step further. We want to pray in agreement with God's plans and purposes. John tells his readers,

> *This is the confidence we have in approaching God: that if we ask anything according to his will, he hears us.* (1 John 5:14)

Again, the place of intimacy—walking with Jesus every day—strengthens our ability to understand what God wants.

PRAY FOR WHAT YOU DO NOT HAVE

Earlier, Jesus predicts the work of the Holy Spirit that will impact future generations after His death. The disciples' grief will turn to joy.

> *In that day, you will no longer ask me anything. I tell you the truth, my Father will give you whatever you ask in my name. Until now, you have not asked for anything in my name. Ask,*

and you will receive, and your joy will be complete. (John 16:23-24)

We miss out because we do not ask:

... you don't have what you want because you don't ask God for it. (NLT James 4:2b)

And even then, our motives must be pure (James 4:3).

HUMILITY AND BOLDNESS

You may know the saying:

"Humility is not thinking less of yourself, it's thinking of yourself less."[1]

We walk in complete surrender to our creator, depending on Him and living with gratitude for His grace. We realise that without Him, we can achieve nothing of spiritual consequence. But we also understand that with God, all things are possible. Humility leads to boldness. Pray the Acts 4:24-31 prayer with confidence.

PRAYING FOR OTHERS

In praying for other people, all these attributes are still relevant. Whoever is receiving prayer wants the ministering person to be confident, use words with power, and bring the life-changing presence of God to bear. We also need a sensitivity to the leading of the Holy Spirit in our prayer ministry.

BIBLICAL EXAMPLES OF PRAYER

We read so many instances of prayer in Scripture. Read the following passages and ask God for pointers that you can incorporate into your own prayer life.

1. The Prayer of Jabez (1 Chronicles 4:10)
2. The Lord's Prayer (Matthew 6:9-13; Luke 11:2-4)
3. Jonah's prayer for salvation (Jonah 2:2-9)
4. David's prayer for deliverance (Psalm 3)
5. Hannah's prayer of petition and praise (1 Samuel 1:10; 2:1-10)
6. Paul's prayer for the Ephesians believers (Ephesians 1:15-23; 3:14-21)

We can easily apply some of these portions of the Bible to our lives. In others, we will need to dig a little to see the heart of the praying person and their particular context.

In your general Bible reading, make a note of prayers. This growing list can aid your own prayer life and help when it is hard to know what to pray. Bible characters are honest and transparent about their feelings and their challenges. Take a brief journey through the Psalms and observe how the writer addresses God, acknowledging the injustices of life. Sometimes, there is a gripe about a clear lack of interest from the Lord. Out of such honesty, prayer and praise eventually flow. There is much we can learn from these ancient writings.

USING SCRIPTURE TO PRAY

As we read the Bible, we can turn phrases and sentences into prayers. We pray for what lies ahead, for our families and our world. It is powerful to pray the words of Scripture. How can we do this? The acronym SOAP may help:

S - Scripture; O - Observation; A - Application; P - Prayer

We read a passage. As we observe its meaning, we may see how Scripture applies to our situation. Then we pray the words of the Bible. Here is a simple example.

Ephesians 4:14 begins, *then we will no longer be infants*. This challenge concludes, in verse 15, *we will in all things grow up into him who is the Head (Christ)*. We note that spiritual maturity is the goal. A prayer follows that we will grow up in Jesus. We carefully read and apply the Bible.

HEALING

God has created us. He loves us and wants the best for us. Sometimes, He goes out of His way to get our attention.

Healing bodies, emotions and memories is powerful—we notice! And so, the loving heavenly Father who delights in relationship with His children draws us. What parent wants anything less?

God heals throughout the Bible. I base the following on some lists of Scripture from a number of people, together with personal study and observations over the years.

GOD REVEALS HIMSELF AS A HEALING GOD

> [The LORD] said, "If you listen carefully to the LORD your God and do what is right in his eyes, if you pay attention to his commands and keep all his decrees, I will not bring on you any of the diseases I brought on the Egyptians, for I am the LORD, who heals you." (Exodus 15:26)

Protection from disease is conditional in this passage. God blesses the Israelites when they are obedient. Nevertheless, He can prevent and heal sickness.

The Psalms pick up this theme, describing God as the one who *heals all your diseases* (103:3) and *heals the broken-hearted and binds up their wounds* (147:3).

HEALING IS A MARK OF THE MESSIAH

From the time of King David, the Israelites looked forward to another ruler. Like David, this *Messiah* figure would restore Israel, though not in the way they expected. Jesus fulfilled this promise and proved it by what He did:

> When [John's disciples] had come to [Jesus], they said, "John the Baptist has sent us to you to ask, 'Are you the one who is to come, or are we to wait for another?'" Jesus had just then cured many people of diseases, plagues, and evil spirits and had given sight to many who were blind. And he answered them, "Go and tell John what you have seen and heard: the blind receive their sight, the lame walk, the lepers are cleansed, the deaf hear, the dead are raised, the poor have good news brought to them." (NRSV Luke 7:20-22)

God's Messiah proved His identity, in part, through His healing.

JESUS CALLS US ALL TO FOLLOW HIM

The Scriptures are clear and challenging on what Jesus expects of His followers. He says:

> "Heal the sick, raise the dead, cleanse those who have leprosy, drive out demons. Freely you have received, freely give." (Matthew 8:10)

Consequently, His disciples:

> Went out and preached that people should repent. They drove out

> *many demons and anointed many sick people with oil and*
> *healed them.* (Mark 6:12-13)

Before His ascension, Jesus instructs His followers to communicate what He taught them:

> *"Therefore go and make disciples of all nations, baptising them in*
> *the name of the Father and of the Son and of the Holy Spirit,*
> *and teaching them to obey everything I have commanded*
> *you."* (Matthew 28:19-20)

THE SCOPE OF GOD'S HEALING

God is unlimited. He is the one who heals all our diseases (Psalm 103:3). And Jesus healed everyone who came to Him:

> *Many followed [Jesus], and he healed all their sick.* (Matthew 12:15b)

It is true Jesus arrived at the house of Lazarus too late to heal him (Luke 11). In that case, there was no need for a healing, but a resurrection would soon take place. This unexpected event is our first introduction to the mystery element of healing. We may also ask why God does not heal everyone? We will consider this further below.

HEALING IN THE KINGDOM OF GOD

In Luke 10:9, the command to heal precedes a claim; *the Kingdom of God is near* those newly healed. This connection appears to validate the Kingdom. At the least, such healing is entirely compatible with the Kingdom rule of God. One sign this Kingdom is taking effect is that healings occur.

GOD AT WORK

Sometimes particular grace is present for miracles of healing to occur:

> *One day as [Jesus] was teaching, Pharisees and teachers of the law ... were sitting there. And the power of the Lord was present for him to heal the sick.* (Luke 5:17)

> *God did extraordinary miracles through Paul ...* (Acts 19:11).

And at other times, there are clear blockages:

> *[In Nazareth, Jesus] could not do any miracles ... except lay his hands on a few sick people and heal them.* (Mark 6:5)

Not everyone finds healing in the ministry of Paul. He tells Timothy that:

> *Erastus stayed in Corinth, and [he] left Trophimus sick in Miletus.* (2 Timothy 4:20)

MOTIVATION

We move in healing because we want to obey Jesus and show compassion to the sick. We do not collect testimonies for our advancement. Our prayers are for the honour of Jesus' name, and it is in that name we pray. Read the prayer of the persecuted disciples in Acts 4:

> *"Stretch out your hand to heal and perform miraculous signs and wonders through the name of your holy servant Jesus."* (Acts 4:30)

GOD USES PEOPLE TO BRING HEALING

Consider the many biblical examples, such as Moses (Numbers 12:13), Elisha (2 Kings 4:18-37), Philip (Acts 8:5-7) and Ananias (Acts 9:10-18). And, of course, this continues today. We are privileged to witness and be used by God in bringing healing. Throughout church history, some disciples continue to believe and trust God to see people healed. He will use you too as you step out and obey Him.

MYSTERY

Sometimes we pray, and there is no recovery. How do we process this disappointment? From experience, I know that this can be very hard. Embracing mystery is vital in our walk with God. That is as true in healing as it is in any other area of life. There is much that we do not understand. We may need to wait for heaven before we receive the answers.

All we must do is remain faithful. God can heal. He will use you and me. So go for it! Leave the results in His hands.

DELIVERANCE

The commission of Jesus includes the deliverance of people from demonic oppression. This reality is often overlooked or delegated to the ministry of a small group of specialists. And yet, it is a thoroughly biblical and essential service to the world in which we live.

We all open ourselves to this oppression when we choose to live outside the boundaries God has provided. The enemy mercilessly exploits these vulnerable areas. He oppresses believers, but the Holy Spirit still indwells us. Non-believers can be totally under the control of the enemy.

WHAT DOES JESUS SAY?

> Jesus called his twelve disciples to him and gave them authority to drive out **impure spirits** and to heal every disease and sickness ... "Heal the sick, raise the dead, cleanse those who have leprosy, drive out **demons**." (Matthew 10:1, 8a)

> [Jesus] appointed twelve that they might be with him and that he might send them out to preach and to have authority to drive

*out **demons**. ... Calling the Twelve to him, he began to send
them out two by two and gave them authority over **impure
spirits** ... They went out and preached that people should
repent. They drove out many **demons** and anointed many
sick people with oil and healed them.* (Mark 3:14-15; 6:7,
12-13)

*When Jesus had called the Twelve together, he gave them power
and authority to drive out all **demons** and to cure diseases. ...
The seventy-two returned with joy and said, "Lord, even the
demons submit to us in your name." He replied, "I saw
Satan fall like lightning from heaven. I have given you
authority to trample on snakes and scorpions and to overcome
all **the power of the enemy**; nothing will harm you.
However, do not rejoice that the **spirits** submit to you, but
rejoice that your names are written in heaven."* (Luke 9:1;
10:17-20)

These words from Jesus to His disciples are clear and powerful
when we list them together. He also calls us, as later followers, to
do the same:

*And these signs will accompany those who believe: In my name,
they will drive out **demons**;* (Mark 16:17a)

PAUL AND JAMES

Both these New Testament writers acknowledge demonic activity:

*No, in all these things we are more than conquerors through him
who loved us. For I am convinced that neither death nor life,
neither angels nor **demons**, neither the present nor the
future, nor any powers, neither height nor depth, nor
anything else in all creation, will be able to separate us from*

the love of God that is in Christ Jesus our Lord. (Romans 8:37-39)

The Spirit clearly says that in later times, some will abandon the faith and follow deceiving spirits and things taught by **demons***.* (1 Timothy 4:1)

You believe that there is one God. Good! Even the **demons** *believe that—and shudder.* (James 2:19)

Paul reminds his readers that demonic oppression is not greater than the love of God expressed in the person of Jesus. And this reality is the foundation of our ability to deal with the demonic.

OUR POSITION

We must appreciate who we are, what Jesus has done and where He seats us:

I pray … that you may know the hope to which he has called you … and his incomparably great power for us who believe. That power is the same as the mighty strength he exerted when he raised Christ from the dead and seated him at his right hand in the heavenly realms, far above all rule and authority, power and dominion, and every name that is invoked, not only in the present age but also in the one to come. And God placed all things under his feet and appointed him to be head … (Ephesians 1:18-23)

And God raised us up with Christ and seated us with him in the heavenly realms in Christ Jesus … (Ephesians 2:6)

Jesus is superior to the enemy. He seats us with Him in heavenly places, and the enemy is under our feet. This truth is vital.

We also understand the enemy is not to be ignored or underestimated. In Acts 19, non-believing Jews attempt an exorcism.

> *Then the man who had the evil spirit jumped on [the Jews] and*
> *overpowered them all. He gave them such a beating that they*
> *ran out of the house naked and bleeding.* (Acts 19:16)

SOME PRACTICALITIES

When we deal with the demonic, we start with our identity in Christ. Motivated by love, we act with the authority we carry and bring people to Jesus. Only He can set them free.

We are mindful of the spiritual opposition arrayed against us, but we need not fear,

> *For the one who is in you is greater than the one who is in the*
> *world.* (1 John 4:4).

You may discern a particular spirit, and if so, you can address it directly. Otherwise, a more general command for the forces of the enemy to leave is sufficient. Remember the power of the blood of Jesus. Once, when praying for someone who sensed they carried an evil presence, they reacted strongly each time I mentioned Jesus' blood.

When it comes to a spiritual force making someone act violently or offensively, we protect the dignity of the individual. That may mean commanding the spirit to leave the person alone. Then we can deal with the situation.

More generally, I prefer the term 'demonised' rather than 'possessed'. It is a better English translation, and reflects the reality that a Jesus follower can be influenced by the enemy but not taken over.

Finally, never be afraid to ask for help. There is no shame in that.

PROPHECY AND WORDS OF KNOWLEDGE

Prophecy is both complex and controversial. It is also a broad topic that deserves a more detailed discussion. Nevertheless, there are general principles that we can glean from Scripture about prophecy and words of knowledge.

The nouns *prophet* and *prophecy* and the verb *prophesy* occur 429 times in the NIV Old Testament and 201 times in the New Testament. Many of these references are to *the prophets*, meaning books of the Old Testament.[1]

PREDICTION

First, predictive prophecy. Agabus was a New Testament prophet. He:

> ... *stood up and, through the Spirit, predicted that a severe famine would spread over the entire Roman world. (This happened during the reign of Claudius).* (Acts 11:28)

Later, he:

> ... *took Paul's belt, tied his own hands and feet with it and said,*

"The Holy Spirit says, 'In this way the Jews of Jerusalem will
bind the owner of this belt and hand him over to the
Gentiles.'" (Acts 21:11)

These are both examples of predictive prophecy, something more often associated with the Old Testament. Think of the prophecies about the coming Messiah (amongst many others, Genesis 3:15 and Isaiah 9:6-7). There is every reason to believe that such predictions would be helpful today. May this be our experience!

SPEAKING TO LEADERS

Another function of the prophetic is to speak truth to power.

Deborah, a prophetess ... sent for Barak ... and said to him, "The
LORD, the God of Israel, commands you ..." (Judges 4:4, 6)

And Samuel tells Saul,

"You have rejected the word of the LORD, and the LORD has
rejected you as king over Israel!" (1 Samuel 15:26)

In the New Testament, Stephen speaks prophetically to the Jewish authorities. No-one gives him the title prophet, but he uses Scripture to drive home his point.

"Brothers and fathers, listen to me! The God of glory appeared to
our father Abraham while he was still in Mesopotamia ..."
(Acts 7:2)

Sadly, power does not always receive the truth. It is also sometimes the case that the speaker is unwise in what is shared, or the manner of sharing. Let us be as careful in the delivery of our message as we are discerning in its reception.

LOCAL CHURCHES TODAY

One key element of New Testament prophecy is to bring a word that builds up, encourages, or brings comfort. After the Jerusalem council in Acts 15, the leaders write to non-Jewish believers. Two prophetic council members carry the letter to Antioch:

> *Judas and Silas, who themselves were prophets, said much to encourage and strengthen the brothers.* (Acts 15:32)

Paul also connects prophetic ministry to encouragement when he writes to the Corinthian followers of Jesus.

> *... everyone who prophesies speaks to men for their strengthening, encouragement and comfort ... he who prophesies edifies the church.* (1 Corinthians 14:3-4)

Wherever and whenever we live, there is a need for such encouragement. Perhaps this is more than simply saying, "well done". That, of course, is important. But in this context, prophecy brings the perspective of God into the present. We allow the voice of God to speak to a person or situation. We act as a channel for the life-changing stream of God. And so God builds up His church.

In contrast to the prophetic function of Ephesians 4:11-12, the passages in Corinthians suggest prophecy is available to the whole body of Christ.

TEACHING AND SPONTANEITY

Prophecy and teaching are distinct gifts, but they may overlap. Daniel clearly understands Scripture and prophesies in that light (Daniel 9:2, 4). Teaching both Bible and doctrine must have a *cutting edge* if it is to be more than sharing information. The need for such prophetic teaching is clear. The application of Scripture to daily life is a prophetic function, and, as teachers, we must bring the *now-word* of God.

The Bible does not address spontaneous versus prepared words of prophecy. Both are acceptable and useful in building up the church. I come from a tradition that championed the spontaneous sharing of Scripture or encouraging the followers of Jesus. But in recent years, I have grown to appreciate written prayers, and the written prophetic statements of Scripture. This is another classic case of *both/and*, rather than *either/or*.

FORGIVENESS

Recently, I listened to a fascinating podcast that featured a former believer who was now a reluctant agnostic. He was supportive of the church but could not understand why followers of Jesus made so little of forgiveness. He thought this belief distinguished the Christian faith from other religions.

FOR EVERYONE

An old song begins

> God forgave my sin in Jesus' name / I've been born again in Jesus' name / And in Jesus' name, I come to you / To share His love as He told me to[1]

> — CAROL OWENS

Forgiveness reflects the heart of God, and we find it shown throughout the Bible. The LORD is the one who:

> *forgives all your sins and heals all your diseases* (Psalm 103:3)

When God's people are in great need, they cry out to Him for forgiveness. After Daniel's vision in chapter eight, he prays:

> "O Lord, listen! O Lord, forgive! O Lord, hear and act! For your sake, O my God, do not delay, because your city and your people bear your Name." (Daniel 9:19)

This verse connects the desire of God to forgive to the honour of His name. He forgives because it is consistent with His character. Forgiveness shouts to a watching world that God loves His people.

And in the New Testament, when the Jewish authorities bring Peter and the other apostles before them, Peter reminds his listeners:

> "The God of our fathers raised Jesus from the dead—whom you had killed by hanging him on a tree. God exalted him to his own right hand as Prince and Saviour that he might give repentance and forgiveness of sins to Israel." (Acts 5:30-31)

FOR INDIVIDUALS

God does not only forgive at the national level, personal forgiveness is also possible.

> If we confess our sins, he is faithful and just and will forgive us our sins and purify us from all unrighteousness. (1 John 1:9)

Sin separates (Romans 3:23), but God connects through His grace and forgiveness. On one level, this is so basic. And yet, forgiveness is profound in its depth and utterly life-changing.

When we celebrate the Lord's Supper, we proclaim that the death of Jesus is enough to reconcile sinful humankind to a holy God. Forgiveness does it all! Under the old covenant,

... without the shedding of blood, there is no forgiveness.
(Hebrews 9:22)

But now,

... the blood of Jesus, [God's] Son, purifies us from sin. (1 John
1:7)

Take a moment and reflect on what forgiveness means to you.

FORGIVING OTHERS

We will all experience broken relationships. This is often a painful
breakdown of trust and communication. Perhaps one party has
wronged the other. And in that case, the only solution is apology
and forgiveness.

The challenge often lies in forgiving someone who has done us
harm, particularly if we have a strong sense of justice. But we
damage ourselves when we refuse to forgive. You may have come
across the saying that not forgiving someone is like drinking
poison and expecting the other person to die.[2] We know from
personal experience the truth of this statement. A lack of forgiveness leads to bitterness and many emotional and physical
problems.

The Lord's prayer mentions forgiveness for others, linking it to
God forgiving us:

"Forgive us our debts, as we also have forgiven our debtors."
(Matthew 6:12).

LINKS TO OTHER AREAS

During times of prayer ministry, it is helpful to ask the person receiving prayer if they need to forgive anyone. In some situations, such forgiveness is all that is necessary to see healing.

Perhaps the greatest challenge is forgiving ourselves. We can be hard on other people, but most of all, on ourselves. Even when we have made serious mistakes, we can apply God's grace, accept His forgiveness and our own, and move on.

Sadly, church is frequently a source of pain. We may need to forgive leaders, congregations, or denominations. When the Lord brings any of this to mind, do not be slow to forgive. It will set you free.

Forgiveness is not an easy topic for many people. If you struggle with it, you are not alone. Bring your reluctance to God and ask for His help. He desires your freedom and will help you make it a reality. Paul wrote to the Galatians about their misunderstanding of the Jewish law. We may face a distinct challenge with forgiveness, but Paul's words are as relevant to us:

> It is for freedom that Christ has set up free. Stand firm, then, and do not let yourselves be burdened again by a yoke of slavery. (Galatians 5:1)

PART IV
OUR LEADING

LEADING YOURSELF AND OTHERS

We always need godly leadership. Some people shy away from the role because they confuse leadership with an organisational position. But leadership is not a job title. It occurs when others follow us for a purpose.

Years ago, I heard of a Chinese proverb which reminds leaders to check if anyone is following them; if not, they are merely going for a walk.[1] Jesus leads His followers. God also calls us to be leaders.

WHAT IS LEADERSHIP?

A local school has adopted and modified a secular definition that is a helpful starting point:

> Leadership is a process of social influence, which positively focuses the efforts of others towards the achievement of a shared aim.[2]

> — KEVIN KRUSE

From a Christian perspective, the influence is spiritual. The shared aim may include several components, but one goal is the growth of the Kingdom of God. We must lead in a godly manner if God's kingdom is our focus.

The view of Jesus is clear.

> *"For even the Son of Man did not come to be served, but to serve, and to give his life as a ransom for many."* (Mark 10:45)

Jesus turns the accepted standards of the world upside down. Earlier in this passage, James and John lobby Jesus for a prominent place in the future kingdom. They want to be first. But Jesus tells them that earthly rulers often progress through knocking others down. Such self-promotion is not the way in the Kingdom of God, and Jesus underlines this in 10:45. If anyone can lead, it is He. Jesus gives up this privilege because His kingdom runs on different principles. He models behaviour that we would do well to follow.

It is hard to respect leaders who claim to be disciples but are autocratic in their dealings with fellow believers.

LEAD YOURSELF.

Paul tells the Thessalonians:

> *Live in peace with each other. And we urge you, brothers and sisters, warn those who are idle and disruptive, encourage the disheartened, help the weak, be patient with everyone. Make sure that nobody pays back wrong for wrong, but always strive to do what is good for each other and everyone else. Rejoice always, pray continually, give thanks in all circumstances; for this is God's will for you in Christ Jesus. Do not quench the Spirit. Do not treat prophecies with*

*contempt but test them all; hold on to what is good, reject
every kind of evil.* (1 Thessalonians 5:13b-22)

Do not aim at perfection, but live with an awareness of who God
is calling you to be. It helps those you lead to see your character,
warts and all.

Maturity is worth pursuing:

> *Consider it pure joy, my brothers and sisters, whenever you face
> trials of many kinds, because you know that the testing of
> your faith produces perseverance. Let perseverance finish its
> work so that you may be mature and complete, not lacking
> anything. If any of you lack wisdom, you should ask God,
> who gives generously to all without finding fault, and it will
> be given to you. But when you ask, you must believe and not
> doubt, because the one who doubts is like a wave of the sea,
> blown and tossed by the wind.* (James 1:2-6)

Life is challenging, but we keep going. We model a dogged persistence that others will follow.

We can refuse to take offence, giving the benefit of the doubt to
others. Much of what seems important now is trivial when we
consider it later. A mature approach wins the day.

LEAD OTHERS.

Leadership comes down to leading people as we wish to be led.
We can be authentic as we show an appropriate vulnerability.
People will connect far more with your failures than your
successes. However, if a leader falls apart consistently, we would
find it hard to follow them.

We must be clear about what we communicate and expect. I have
found that people rise to the level of my expectation. This is true
for all ages. Sometimes, we can be confident in another person

when they are not confident in themselves. Our belief in a follower of Jesus spurs them on. After all, if God can use me, He can use anyone!

Look for opportunities to lead. Be open to sharing what God has done in your life. Have a generous heart. And even if others never call you 'leader', they will follow you and become more like Jesus.

LOVING GOD WELL

What do we mean when we claim to love God well? God provides a clue in the books of Leviticus, Deuteronomy and Mark:

> [God:] *"You shall not take vengeance or bear a grudge against any of your people, but you shall love your neighbour as yourself: I am the LORD."* (NRSV Leviticus 19:18)

> [Moses:] *"Hear, O Israel: The LORD is our God, the LORD alone. You shall love the LORD your God with all your heart, and with all your soul, and with all your might."* (NRSV Deuteronomy 6:4-5)

Jesus brings these texts together in Mark 12.

> *One of the scribes came near and heard them disputing with one another, and seeing that he answered them well, he asked him, "Which commandment is the first of all?" Jesus answered, "The first is, 'Hear, O Israel: the Lord our God, the Lord is one; you shall love the Lord your God with all your heart, and with all your soul, and with all your mind, and with all your strength.' The second is this, 'You shall love your neighbour*

*as yourself.' There is no other commandment greater than
these."* (NRSV Mark 12:28-31)

Jewish rabbis sought a single, unifying principle that would
summarise the 613 commandments of the Pentateuch.[1] More
recently, Einstein searched for a *theory of everything* in the 1920s,
and physicist Stephen Hawking discussed this in his book, *A Brief
History of Time*.[2] The idea of a summary of all that is important is
not new.

God encourages the Israelites to love Him with their whole being
—heart, soul and might. Today, we may use the terms body, soul,
and spirit.

SACRED AND SECULAR DIVIDE.

It is easy to separate our lives into what we term *sacred* and *secular*
categories. Church attendance may fall in the first grouping and
home life in the second. But to God, every part of our lives is
sacred.

> *And whatever you do, whether in word or deed, do it all in the
> name of the Lord Jesus, giving thanks to God the Father
> through him.* (Colossians 3:17)

If we struggle to do something in the name of Jesus, perhaps we
should stop.

However, if we refuse to artificially separate our lives, we find
God is more interested in us than we imagine. We can invite His
participation in everything. We have often asked God for strategies to cope well during challenging seasons. God cares, and if we
involve Him in the totality of our lives, then we can love Him in
the same way.

BODY, SOUL AND SPIRIT

We love God well when we take care of our bodies. Many well-known people have died young, including the Scottish pastor Robert Murray McCheyne. He died at twenty-nine, and whether the saying attributed to him is accurate, the sentiment holds true:

> "The Lord gave me a horse to ride and a message to deliver. Alas, I have killed the horse and cannot deliver the message."[3]

— ATTRIBUTED TO ROBERT MURRAY M'CHEYNE

Our bodies are more important than we realise. Diet and exercise are key indicators of our health. Many of us have bought in to an old Gnostic heresy that body and soul belong to people's earthly existence and are of less value than spirit. We argue that 'spiritual' matters should be our focus and what we do with our bodies is secondary.

This is so wrong. The psalmist is clear that we are

fearfully and wonderfully made (Psalm 139:14)

and Paul rejects the notion that the body is inconsequential (1 Corinthians 6:12-20).

We can ask God for strategies to steward our bodies well. Since everyone has a finite life, as followers of Jesus, we want to use our lives wisely. This requires discipline, and the rewards are huge. Healthy bodies positively impact our minds and emotions, as well as our spiritual lives. Sometimes, it is as simple as getting enough sleep, eating a healthy diet and regularly exercising.

Learning to say 'no' is a skill that will impact our bodies, minds and spirits. It is easy to become physically and emotionally over-loaded because of constant demands, some of which are unreasonable. For many, saying 'no' is incredibly difficult, and all of us will need to work on it continually. We may not be present at every meeting or join every team. But we will get involved in everything that God wants. This may be a major departure from our previous lifestyle. But it will be one in which we do not burn out. We serve God as marathon runners, not sprinters. God has given us,

> ... *a spirit of power, of love, and of self-discipline.* (2 Timothy
> 1:7)

We can do this! Perhaps this is a challenge, but God has called us to:

> ... *not conform any longer to the pattern of this world, but be
> transformed by the renewing of [our minds]. Then [we] will
> be able to test and approve what God's will is—his good,
> pleasing and perfect will.* (Romans 12:2)

As God's Spirit fills us (Ephesians 5:18), our spirit connects with Him. We understand God calls us to thrive, not merely survive. When our bodies, souls and spirits are healthy, we love Him with our whole being. There is no divide between the sacred and the secular.

PART V
MOVING FORWARD

WHEN THE GOING GETS TOUGH

Life can be stretching. The challenges may derail us unless we expect this reality and put into place strategies to deal with what comes our way.

WHAT DOES THE BIBLE SAY?

We are fortunate that many biblical passages help us keep going when the going gets tough. Consider the following verses, ask God for His insight, and make a note of what you can use. We face practical problems. God offers practical solutions.

Let's be real! This is what Jesus says to us:

> "In this world, you will have trouble. But take heart! I have overcome the world." (John 16:33)

Paul tells the Christ followers in Colosse and Philippi:

> Since you have been raised to new life with Christ, set your sights on the realities of heaven, where Christ sits in the place of honour at God's right hand. Think about the things of heaven, not the things of earth. For you died to this life, and

your real life is hidden with Christ in God. And when Christ,
who is your life, is revealed to the whole world, you will share
in all his glory ... Let the message about Christ, in all its
richness, fill your lives. Teach and counsel each other with all
the wisdom he gives. Sing psalms and hymns and spiritual
songs to God with thankful hearts. And whatever you do or
say, do it as a representative of the Lord Jesus, giving thanks
through him to God the Father. (NLT Colossians 3:1-4,
16-17)

I pray that your love will overflow more and more, and that you
will keep on growing in knowledge and understanding. For I
want you to understand what really mattered, so that you
may live pure and blameless lives until the day of Christ's
return. May you always be filled with the fruit of your
salvation - the righteous character produced in your life by
Jesus Christ - for this will bring much glory and praise to
God. (NLT Philippians 1:9-11)

In the Old Testament,

For you are my hiding place; you protect me from trouble. You
surround me with songs of victory. ... Unfailing love
surrounds those who trust the LORD. *So rejoice in the* LORD
and be glad, all you who obey him! Shout for joy, all you
whose hearts are pure. (NLT Psalm 32:7, 10, 11)

[Hannah says,] "My heart rejoices in the LORD! *The* LORD *has*
made me strong. Now I have an answer for my enemies; I
rejoice because you rescued me. No one is holy like the LORD!
There is no one besides you: there is no Rock like our God."
(NLT 1 Samuel 2:1-2)

When King David loses the trust of his men, he

Was greatly distressed because the men were talking about
stoning him; each one was bitter in spirit because of his sons
and daughters. But David found strength in the LORD his
God. (1 Samuel 30:6)

As a general rule, our situations are not as dire as David's, but
God remains the source of all that we need. In fact,

God has said, "I will never fail you. I will never abandon you."
So we can say with confidence, "The Lord is my helper, so I
will have no fear. What can mere people do to me?" (NLT
Hebrews 13:5-6)

We can find many more passages that speak of God's provision
for us. In particular, the Psalms record human emotion and
response to trying circumstances. If you are in need, read through
this remarkable book until you hear God speak to your heart.
Look at Psalms 23, 37, 55, 56, 61 and 91, just to get started.

GOD'S STRATEGY.

Take time and ask God for a 'strategy plan' when faced with trials.
Be intentional. Do not expect everything to fall into place, but be
prepared. God has given us everything we need. It is our role to
take what He has provided and use it.

NEXT STEPS

Where do we go from here? Gathering information is helpful, but not enough. We must act on what we know.

Find like-minded people who wish to move forward with you. This is so important. They will be fellow disciples who understand everyone has much still to learn. They also yearn for meaningful community.

Here, we can be ourselves without fear, confident that others want what is best for us all. This will be a place to learn from one another, to have fun together, and to see Jesus change us, one day at a time.

This community may arise in an existing church or fellowship group, or may require a new venture. Either way, ask God for His initiatives.

> *If it is possible, as far as it depends on you, live at peace with everyone.* (Romans 12:18)

Unity is always a goal that God blesses (Psalm 133). However, when we confuse unity and uniformity, some people exert unhelpful pressure. Unity is togetherness, a shared vision and passion that leads us forward. Uniformity is the pressure to believe or behave in some standard manner.

So, find others who will go on a journey with Jesus and with you. We have no predetermined destination. We are not even clear about what we will face on the way. It is the journeying which counts, the travelling companions who will spur you on.

Enjoy the adventure!

> So: to the one who is capable of doing far, far more than we can ask or imagine, granted the power which is working in us—to him be glory, in the church, and in King Jesus, to all generations, and to the ages of ages! Amen! (NTE Ephesians 3:20-21)

RESOURCES

FURTHER READING

With every book other than the Bible, we encourage people to read with a discerning eye. "Chew the meat and spit out the bones!" This book has referred to the publications listed below, but the list also contains further helpful material.

Mark Batterson, *The Circle Maker* (Grand Rapids, MI; Zondervan, 2012).

Oswald Chambers, *My Utmost for His Highest: An Updated Edition in Today's Language* (Grand Rapids, MI; Discovery House, 1992).

Ken Fleming, *Peter Fleming: A Man of Faith* (Spring Lake, NJ: CMML, 1995).

Billy Graham, *The Holy Spirit: Activating God's Power in Your Life* (Nashville, TN: Thomas Nelson, 1978/1988).

Wayne Grudem, *Systematic Theology: An Introduction to Biblical Doctrine* (Leicester: Inter-Varsity Press, 1994).

Patricia King, *Decree a thing, and it shall be established* (Maricopa, AZ: XP Publishing, 3rd edition 2012).

Margaret Nagib, *Sozo for Professional Counsellors: Integrating Psychology and Inner Healing to Restore Individuals to Wholeness* (Self-published, 2013).

Watchman Nee, *The Spiritual Man* (New York, NY: Christian Fellowship Publishers, Inc., 1968).

Leonard Ravenhill, *Why Revival Tarries* (Minneapolis, MN: Bethany Fellowship, 1959).

Rob Rufus, *Living in the Grace of God* (London: Authentic Media, 1997).

John Sandford and Mark Sandford, *A Comprehensive Guide to Deliverance and Inner Healing* (Grand Rapids: Baker Books, 1992).

Jonathan and Paige Squirrell, *Thrive* (Kingdom Breakthrough, 2019).

Paige Squirrell, *Captivated by His Beauty* (Kingdom Breakthrough, 2017).

———, *Songs from the Father* (Kingdom Breakthrough, 2018).

———, *Whispers from Heaven* (Kingdom Breakthrough, 2017).

A. W. Tozer, *The Knowledge of the Holy: The Attributes of God: Their Meaning in the Christian Life* (London: James Clarke & Co., 1961).

Kris Vallotton and Bill Johnson, *The Supernatural Ways of Royalty* (Shippensburg, PA: Destiny Image, 2006).

Mark and Patti Virkler, *4 Keys to Hearing God's Voice* (Shippensburg, PA: Destiny Image, 2010).

KINGDOM BREAKTHROUGH

Connect with us through **kingdombreakthrough.org**. There are several written resources available. If there are any practical ways in which we can encourage you, please get in touch.

AFTERWORD

Topics covered in the preceding chapters impact both individuals and groups of Jesus followers. As we walk with the Spirit of God, each of us has the potential to not only know His power, but also to release it to others.

Our world needs recalibrated disciples who will demonstrate the power of the Kingdom of God. Words alone are not enough. We shape our circle of influence in many ways, but one of the most powerful is through prayer.

Prayer ministry, or praying for others, is a key weapon in our armoury. Such prayer may be long distance, on the phone or through video chat. Miracles are not restricted by distance. But when possible, I encourage you to pray for others when you are with them. You will find the immediacy of spiritual warfare exhilarating, occasionally nerve-wracking, and always worthwhile.

When we pray in this manner, we invite the presence of God into a person's life. The Father was never absent, of course, but moments of particular connection can yield huge dividends. God's presence is always a blessing. In that sense, to pray is to succeed. Every time we pray, we open the door for God to work.

We also understand that often there are particular outcomes in mind. Those who are sick or injured desire healing; the bereaved cry out for God's comfort; and those desperate for God to break through in deliverance or provision need to see Him move.

In these cases, ask the person what they are seeking. It may not be obvious. Spend time with them, asking God how He sees the situation in front of you. And then pray! Be direct, address the issue with godly confidence as a child of the King. Where appropriate, ask whether there is any change. In praying for healing, I almost always question whether the condition is better, worse, or unchanged. This gives someone permission to admit that all is as it was. Worsening conditions may indicate a spiritual root to the physical problem.

When breakthrough is not complete (or present at all), pray again. Then, re-interview. We can so easily be discouraged and give up. Once I prayed eight times for a back problem before there was any improvement. We pray until God breaks through or we sense we have prayed enough.

In some cases, praying once is all we need to do—the prayer for a job, or financial provision, for example.

When God answers prayer, do not be surprised...

Our Father delights to use His children. And that means you.

So step out of the boat, trust God, believe what He says about you, and be the answer to the unspoken prayers of an empty world. You can shape your culture more than you realise. And when you see God move in these wonderful ways, contact me and let me know.

Cheering you on and believing in you.

Jonathan

NOTES

INTRODUCTION

1. Leonard Ravenhill, *Why Revival Tarries* (Minneapolis, MN: Bethany Fellowship, 1959).
2. Robin Marks, "All for Jesus" (Copyright 1990, Word Music).

3. LEADERSHIP

1. Bill Hybels, *Courageous Leadership* (Grand Rapids. MI: Zondervan; 2002), p. 3.

7. THE LANGUAGE OF THE SPIRIT

1. Mark and Patti Virkler, *4 Keys to Hearing God's Voice* (Shippensburg, PA: Destiny Image, 2010).

8. THE WORD OF GOD

1. Wayne Grudem, *Systematic Theology: An Introduction to Biblical Doctrine* (Leicester: Inter-Varsity Press, 1994), pp. 47-50.

9. JESUS OUR MODEL

1. Reading for 5 March from Oswald Chambers, *My Utmost for His Highest: An Updated Edition in Today's Language* (Grand Rapids, MI; Discovery House, 1992).
2. See also Mark 6:46, John 15:1-17 and Revelation 3:20.
3. See Matthew 9:36; 14:14; 15:32 and 20:34.

11. LIVING AS SONS AND NOT ORPHANS

1. Adapted from Patricia King, *Decree a thing, and it shall be established* (Maricopa, AZ: XP Publishing, 3rd edition 2012), pp. 15-19.

12. INNER HEALING: BACKGROUND

1. Genesis 1:26; 9:6.
2. Watchman Nee, *The Spiritual Man* (New York, NY: Christian Fellowship Publishers, Inc., 1968), p. 29.
3. Margaret Nagib, *Sozo for Professional Counsellors: Integrating Psychology and Inner Healing to Restore Individuals to Wholeness* (Self-published, 2013), p. 59.
4. See Nagib, pp. 65-67.
5. Nagib, pp. 70-71.

13. INNER HEALING: OUTWORKING

1. John Sandford and Mark Sandford, *A Comprehensive Guide to Deliverance and Inner Healing* (Grand Rapids: Baker Books, 1992), p.51.
2. Hebrew 2:18; 2 Corinthians 1:.
3. Psalm 18:29; Philippians 2:13; 4:13.
4. R. Ammi in *Shab. 55a* (Babylonian Talmud).

14. COURAGE

1. https://dictionary.com (accessed 10 July 2021).
2. Merriam-Webster dictionary.
3. https://lexico.com (accessed 10 July 2021).
4. https://www.challengedathletes.org/courage-essay/ (accessed 10 July 2021).
5. 1 John 4:18; John 15.
6. Corrie Ten Boom. *Jesus is Victor* (Grand Rapids, MI: Revell, 1984), p. 183.

15. REVELATION

1. See Chapter 7 above.

17. CULTURE OF HONOUR

1. Kris Vallotton and Bill Johnson, *The Supernatural Ways of Royalty* (Shippensburg, PA: Destiny Image, 2006), p. 118.

19. GRACE

1. Rob Rufus, *Living in the Grace of God* (London: Authentic Media, 1997), pp. xi-xii.
2. Rob Rufus, *Living in the Grace of God* (London: Authentic Media, 1997), p. 18.

3. Terry Virgo, quoted on Andrew Warnock's blog (https://www.patheos.com/blogs/adrianwarnock/2008/09/battling-bitterness-during-tough-times/) accessed July 2021.

21. RESPONDING TO GOD'S CALL

1. Ken Fleming, *Peter Fleming: A Man of Faith* (Spring Lake, NJ: CMML, 1995), pp. 144-145.

22. AUTHORITY AND POWER

1. Billy Graham, *The Holy Spirit: Activating God's Power in Your Life* (Nashville, TN: Thomas Nelson, 1978/1988), p. 295.

23. BUILDING WITH KINGDOM TOOLS

1. A.W. Tozer, *The Knowledge of the Holy: The Attributes of God: Their Meaning in the Christian Life* (London: James Clarke & Co., 1961), p. 9.
2. Reading for 30 November from Oswald Chambers, *My Utmost for His Highest: An Updated Edition in Today's Language* (Grand Rapids, MI; Discovery House, 1992).

25. EFFECTIVE PRAYER

1. Sometimes attributed to CS Lewis, used by Rick Warren in The Purpose Driven Life, but its origin is unclear.

28. PROPHECY AND WORDS OF KNOWLEDGE

1. The Hebrew Scriptures (our Old Testament), is divided into three primary sections: the Law, the Prophets and the Writings.

29. FORGIVENESS

1. Carol Owens, 1974
2. Source unknown.

30. LEADING YOURSELF AND OTHERS

1. Source unknown.
2. Based on a definition by Kevin Kruse in *What is Leadership?* (Forbes Magazine, 9 April, 2013).

31. LOVING GOD WELL

1. The Old Testament books of Genesis, Exodus, Leviticus, Numbers and Deuteronomy.
2. Stephen Hawking, *A Brief History of Time* (London: Bantam Books, 1988)
3. Source unknown.

ABOUT JONATHAN

Jonathan Squirrell works with individuals and groups to encourage spiritual maturity and breakthrough, to support re-evaluation of current church practice, and to champion discipleship in meaningful community.

Jonathan has been married to Paige since 1989 and together they wrote and delivered a curriculum for discipleship that he has repurposed and expanded in this book.

Contact Jonathan through kingdombreakthrough.org.

amazon.com/author/jonathansquirrell

OTHER KINGDOM BREAKTHROUGH BOOKS

BY JONATHAN

Recalibrate Workbook (Paperback)

* * *

WITH PAIGE

Thrive (Paperback)

Thrive (eBook)

* * *

BY PAIGE

Whispers from Heaven (Paperback)

Whispers from Heaven (eBook)

Songs from the Father (Paperback)

Songs from the Father (eBook)

Printed in Great Britain
by Amazon